# Physical and Human Geography of Bundelkhand

# Physical and Human Geography of Bundelkhand

**Dr. Pawan Kumar**

Assistant Professor
Bundelkhand Degree College
Jhansi (Uttar Pradesh)

**Raj Publications**

**New Delhi - 110002**

**Physical and Human Geography of Bundelkhand**



First Published in 2021

**₹ 550**

**ISBN 978-81-950808-4-7**



*Published by* : **Raj Publications**

**108, 4855/24, Ansari Road,**

**Daryaganj, New Delhi - 110002**

**Tel. : 9811010939**

**Email: rajpublications@yahoo.co.in**

*Laser Typesetting* : Ankita Graphics, Delhi

Printed at : Balaji Offset, Navin Shahdra, Delhi-32

The book is dedicated to My Parents

Shri Kamta Prasad &

Smt. Mithlesh Kumari

# Contents

# Preface

The present monograph on Bundelkhand region is a humble contribution to the applied geography. Virtually the region lies in the heart land of the country. The land embracs southern part of Uttar Pradesh and northern Part of Madhya Pradesh consisting thirteen districts with seventy thousand $km^2$ geographical area covers with 1.83 crore population. (2011).

The region has remained under developed by all means due to its physical barriers and cultural traditions up to the sovereignty of Chandela Rajputs. Although Bundelkhand has a unique geographical personality with the strategie importance in the central India. The northern part of Bundelkhand is more developed due to its rich resources and productivity than the Southern undulating topography and poor economy. These are the main hurdles in the way of socio-economic progress of the land.

Furtunatly, the author feels pleasure to write on a neglected part of India in a comprehensive scale about habitat, economy and society of the region is rich in sufficient natural and the human resources. For the socio-economic development of the area these resources could not be utilised to a great extent.

After independence the abolition of zamindari system have changed the social and economic life of the people. Both the state goverment have introduced a several regional development schemes for the welfare of the regional people under the successive five year plans but, these have not achieved the target due to ignorance and illiteracy. In the modern era, Bundelkhand divison urgently needs a full status of Province for the integrated development of the land and the people.

**-- Dr. Pawan Kumar**

# Physical Geography

# 1

# Introduction

## 1. Geographical Background

As understood by the state governments of Uttar Pradesh and Madhya Pradesh Bundelkhand comprises sen district of southern up and seven district of northern M.P. Lalitpur, Jhansi, Jalaun, Hamirpur, Mahoba, Banda, Chitrakoot (U.P.) and Datiya, Tikamgarh, Chhatarpur, Panna, Sagar, Damoh, Niwari and proposed Gwalior and Satna District.

The above delineation is different from boundries suggested by property a greater or cultural Bundelkhand who include many more districts of MP. However the definition used by the UP and M.P. Governments is the most useful from a practical view point this definition is also generally used by the median civil society organizations when they refer to Bundelkhand. The listing of up Bundelkhand district is derived from the scope of the Bundelkhand Vikas Nidhi set up by the UP Government in 1990-91. The listing of M.P. Bundelkhand districts is derived from the scope of the M.P Bundelkhand Development authorty April 2007.

The boundry of Bundelkhand region of defined are

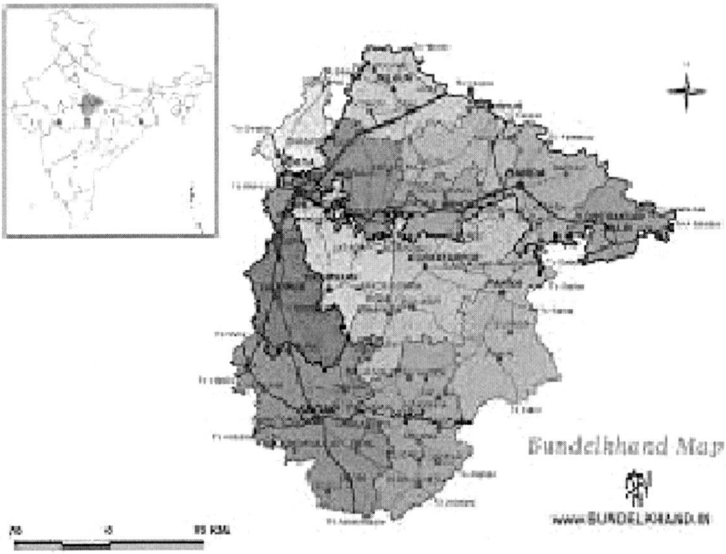


1. In the north Yamuna and Ganga plain.
2. In the east of Vindhyan hills and Panna, Ajaygarh ranges.
3. In the west the Sindh and Chambal rivers, and the Malwa and Udaypur Gwalior regions.
4. In the south, the Narmada and tributaries of the Ken and Betwa.
5. In the south and east, the Vindhyachal and Bundelkhand regions.

**Location of Bundelkhand (in Area ($Km^2$))**

Lalitpur - $24^0$ 11′ N – $25^0$ 14′ N Latitude, $78^0$ 10′ – $79^0$ 01 E Longitude

Jhansi - $25^0$ 43′ N Latitude, $78^0$ 56′ E Longitude

Jalaun - $26^0$ 12′ N Latitude, $79^0$ 47′ E Longitude

Hamirpur - $31^0$ 57′ N Latitude, $76^0$ 50′ E Longitude

| | | |
|---|---|---|
| Mahoba | - | 25° 17' N Latitude, 79° 52' E Longitude |
| Banda | - | 25° 45' N Latitude, 80° 54' E Longitude |
| Chitrakoot | - | 25° 16' N Latitude, 81° 07' E Longitude |
| Datiya | - | 25° 58' N Latitude, 78° 56' E Longitude |
| Damoh | - | 23° 57' N Latitude, 79° 52' E Longitude |
| Tikamgarh | - | 24° 56' N Latitude, 78° 52' E Longitude |
| Chhatarpur | - | 24° 06' - 25° 20' N Latitude, 78° 59' - 80° 56' E Longitude |
| Panna | - | 24° 48' N Latitude, 80° 18' E Longitude |
| Sagar | - | 23° 59' N Latitude, 78° 53' E Longitude |
| Niwari | - | 24° 26' - 25° 40' N Latitude, 78° 26' - 79° 26' E Longitude |
| Gwalior | - | 26° 22' N Latitude, 78° 18' E Longitude |
| Satna | - | 23° 58' - 25° 12' N Latitude, 80° 21' - 81° 23' E Longitude |

## 2. Historical Background

Bundelkhand Historic Region Central India, Not included in Northern Madhya Pradesh, Comprising the Hilly Vindhyan region. Cut by ravines and the North eastern plain, steep, insulated kill rising abruptly from the plains have provided excellent sites for castles and strongholds of Bundelkhand mountaineers, the Dhasan Tons, Ken and Betwa, rivers in deep ravine, fringed, channels are of little use for irrigation though and Betwa River has been dammed and provides, irrigation waters and hydro electricity, Diamonds of good quality, though small in size are found, particularly near Panna, wheat, grain sorghum and cotton are the principal crops.

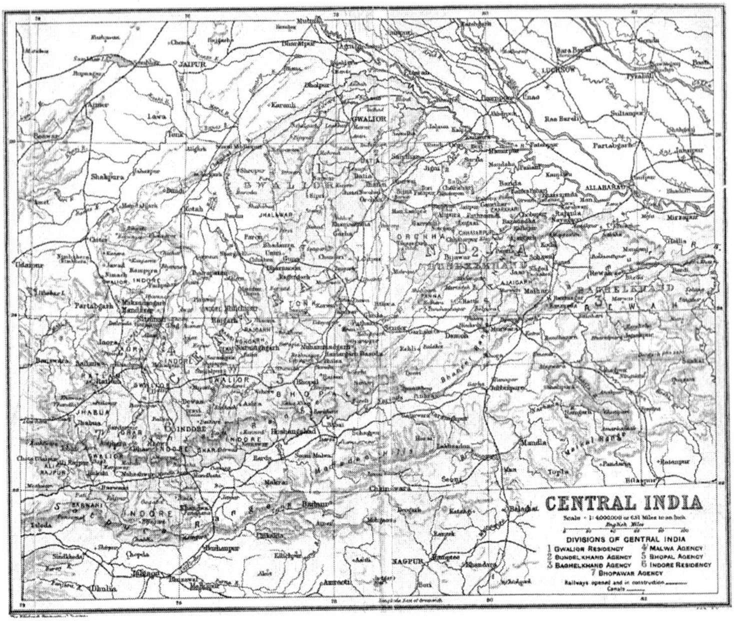


The Galarwars the earliest recorded dynasty Bundelkhand or Jejakabhukti, were succeeded by the Pratihara Rajputs (warry) cast the lotter were supplimanted about 800 CE by the Chandelas, who by the 11 century heldsway over a large territory between the Yamuna and Narwada rivers, the chandelas were over thrown in 1182 by Prithviraja, Ruler of Ajmer and Delhi, after aperiod of ruinous a narchy, Bundela Rajputs (for when the country is named began to settle there in the 14th century) and for centuries afterwards they engaged in guerrilla warfare against the muslim power of Delhi in 1545 Sher Shah Suri, who had defeated the mughal emperor. Humayun invaded Bundelkhand but lost his life while besieging the fortress of Kalinjar. In 1569 Kalinjar surrendered to the forces of the mughal emperor Akbar, with the declined of the mughals. The Marathas extended their influence and in 1792 were acknowledged the as lards of Bundelkhand in 1803. The Districts of Dandy and Hamirpur were transferred to the British and by the treaty of Pune (Poona 1817). The British government acquired from the Marathas all territorial rights over the region.

Historically, Bundelkhand included several districts that are now in Uttar Pradesh, Prior the 1947. However, the Name was restricted politically to the princely states of the Bundelkhand Agency, created in 1802 as a sub agency of the British central India, Agency in 1948 Baghelkhand and Bundelkhand merged into Vindhya Prakas, which, with several former enclaves of southern Uttar Pradesh, merged with Madhya Pradesh in 1956. Bundelkhand thus no longer has any political indentity.

### 3. Political Background

The Marathas ceded part of Bundelkhand, which were later called British Bundelkhand to the British in the 1802 Treaty of Bassein the sanad states were organised into the Bundelkhand. Agency in 1811, when a political agent to the Governor. General of India was appointed and headquarters tired at Banda.

Separated states, Orchha. (1501) Datia, Panna (1732) Ajaygarh (1765) Historical Capitals Khajuraho, Mahoba, Orchha, Garh Kundar. The Bundelkhand Agency was a political agency of the British Raj, managing the relations of the British government with the Protected Princely states of the Bundelkhand Region.

## 4. Cultural Background

Bundelkhand is geographical and cultural region and also a mountain range in central & North India the hilly region is now divided between the state of uttar Pradesh and Madhya Pradesh with the large Portion lying in the letter state.

**Seperate Sates -**

1. Orchha 2. Datia 3. Panna 4. Ajaygarh 5. Bijawar

## Historical Capital

1. Khajuraho 2. Mahoba 3. Orchha 4. Garh Kundar

Bundelkhand lies in the central part of India, embracing south-western Uttar Pradesh and North-western Madhya Pradesh between the Ganga Plain in the north and the Vindhyan land in the south.

It has a complex geologic build. There are four geological systems. The first, Archaean system composed of crystalline igneous and metamorphic rocks. The Bundelkhand gneisses and granites cover an area of about 14000 Kms. The second, the transitional system represents the sedimentary strate of sand stones and limestone in which the lava flows, intrusions penetrates the rocks. Both the Gwalior and Bijawar series are rich in mineral deposits. The third, the Vindhyan system, is semi-circle in the region except from the north. Besides the Panna diamonds, the system is rich in building stones like sandstones and limestones. The last, alluvium land is very fertile for agricultural uses.

It is characterised by a rugged and undulating topography which gives it a distinct entity of natural isolation, stagnation and backwardness. Extensive patches of land are mostly forested, sparsely populated and occupied by dispersed human settlements. The Vindhyan tableland is essentially dissected plateau which is cut deep gorges and precipitous rocky banks by the Betwa, the Dhasan and the Ken. The table land is rich in flora and fauna but poor in means of livelihood resources. The transitional granitic land carries both the plain and plateau physiographic characteristics. The country is frequently criss-crossed by the quartz reefs and dolerite dykes. The large chunk of waste lands and hills has barred the human progress due to the less fertile red soils and lack of irrigational facilities.

The trans-Yamuna plain is divided by the Sind, the Betwa and the Ken into three micro-regions e.g., Jalaun plain, Hamirpur plain and Banda plain. Agriculturally it is very fertile part of Bundelkhand where dry and irrigated farmings is being practiced. The ravine belt along the main streams is badly broken and eroded by innumerable torrents. The rough landscape and stunted bushy vegetal cover provide ample opportunities for stock rearing.

# 2

# Physical Morphology

## Location and Area

Bundelkhand occupies the heartland of India, consisting of the southern part of Uttar Pradesh and northern part of Madhya Pradesh. Its location in medieval period had a unique strategic importance. In the days of political upheaval (12 Cent. A.D. to 17 Cent. A.D.), it was known as the 'gateway to south India'. All the main routes to Deccan Plateau from the Gangetic plain passed through the region. Owing to this fact all the invaders and indigenous rulers were anxious to capture this strategic area. Geographically Bundelkhand lies between the Ganga plain in the north, the Vindhyas in the south, Baghelkhand in the east and the Gwalior and Malwa regions in the north-west. It lies between $24^0.5'$ to $26^030'$ N. Lat. and $78^010'$ E to $81^030'$ E long. Its maximum east-west length is about 370 kms and north-south width about 250 kms. The region commands an area of about 70847 sq. kms.

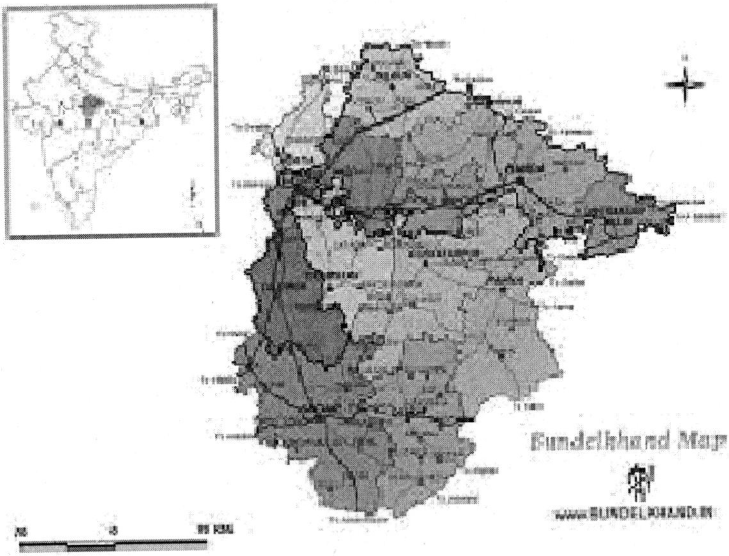


## Table-1

### Area and Population (2011)

| District | Area ($Km^2$) | Total Population | Density Per $Km.^2$ |
|---|---|---|---|
| Lalitpur | 5039 | 12,21,592 | 242 |
| Jhansi | 5024 | 19,98,603 | 398 |
| Jalaun | 4565 | 16,89,974 | 370 |
| Hamirpur | 4021 | 11,04,285 | 275 |
| Mahoba | 3144 | 8,75,958 | 278 |
| Banda | 4408 | 17,99,410 | 402 |
| Chitrakoot | 3216 | 9,91,730 | 308 |
| Datia | 2995 | 7,86,375 | 292 |

| Tikamgarh | 3885 | 10,40,113 | 286 |
|---|---|---|---|
| Chhatarpur | 8687 | 17,62,852 | 203 |
| Panna | 7135 | 10,16,028 | 142 |
| Sagar | 10252 | 23,78,295 | 272 |
| Damoh | 7306 | 12,63,703 | 173 |
| Niwari | 1170 | 4,04,807 | 296 |
| Gwalior | 4560 | 20,32,636 | 446 |
| Satna | 7502 | 22,28,935 | 297 |

We, however, differ from the above views. An attempt has been made to define the area of study mainly on the basis of geomorphic homogeneity, structural unity and climatic uniformity which comprises the basis cultural unity of Bundelkhand. It follows the natural guide-lines which distinguish it from the adjacent areas in geologic structure and physiographic make-up. There is no dispute regarding the northern boundary of the region which coincides with the Yamuna from north-west to south-east. In the west and north-west its boundary is formed by the Betwa and the Sindh rivers. Incidentally the Chandela Empire never extended beyond this line. In the south Lalitpur plateau and Bijawar series demarcated the boundary line of the region. Further, in the south-east the skirts of the region runs along the Panna and Vindhyachal ranges separating the region from the Baghelkhand.

# 3

# Geomorphology

Geomorphology influences in many ways both the natural and cultural environment. This is because the nature of the rocks plays an important role in determining the human activities, the social characteristics, type of farming and settlement patterns. In the areas of hard rocks the human progress has been hampered due to lack of livelihood resources. In the boulder and quartz reef areas where the intensive agriculture is impossible, therefore people are busy in quarrying, mining and other allied activities.

The geological formation of Bundelkhand rocks can be grouped into four main systems :-

(1) The Archaean system : Bundelkhand gneisses and granites.

(2) The Transitional system :

(a) The Gwalior series,

(b) The Bijawar series,

(3) The Vindhyan System :

(i) Upper Vindhyan

(a) Bhander series,

(b) Rewah series

(c) Kaimur series

(ii) Lower Vindhyan

(4) The Recent Deposits : (Trans Yamuna alluvial Plain.)

## 1. The Bijawar Series

The name 'Bijawar' was given by Medlicott in 1859 as the Bijawar series lies in the Bijawar Tahsil of Chhatarpur district. The sediments are found above the Bundelkhand granites and below the lower Vindhyan beds. The Bijawar

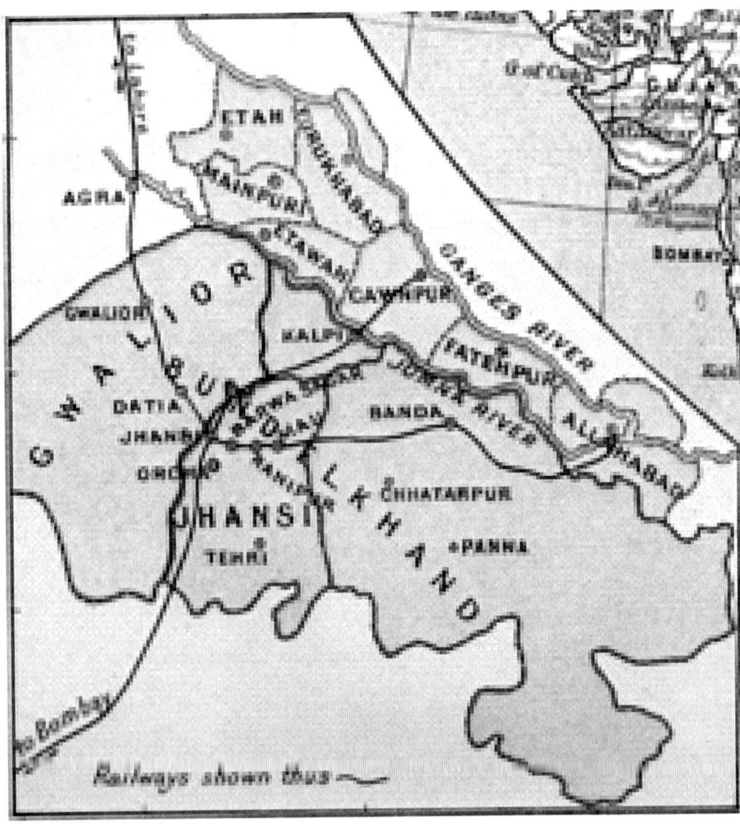

Series is extensively disturbed towards the east. It is totally cut off by the lower Vindhyan and overlap on the older granite. In the eastern side it is divided into two main parts, viz., the lower part consists of conglomerate, quartzite, jaspers cherts, limestones and sandstones, together with inter-bedded lava flows. And the upper part contains ferruginous conglomerates, shales and crushed quartzites together with a horizon of glacial tillite. The total thickness of the bottom rocks of the Bijawar series no where exceeds 70 to 216 meters. The bounded rocks of the series are not similar to Dharwar rocks but the percentage of iron ore is high in both the series. Bijawar and Gwalior from the very beginning both the series were famous for iron ore deposites which were exploited by Bundela chiefs.

## 2. The Vindhyan System

In the Algonkian age, about 600 to 700 million years ago, there was an ancient geosyncline, called the 'Vindhyan Sea' in which the sediments from the ancient Aravalli ranges were deposited. The present evidence of fluvio marine deposits indicates the remoteness of the geological time. The two powerful forces had reacted in the formation of the Vindhyachal and Bhander ranges - one tectonic movement came from west and another isostatic adjustment from south.

The undisturbed and horizontally bedded sediments of Vindhyan system are broadly classified into two divisions :-

(i) Upper Vindhyan and

(ii) Lower Vindhyan

The Upper Vindhyan system is constituted of 'relict structures due to the sculpturing of a basin of sedimentary rocks in which a series of hard sandstones play an important part'. In lower Vindhyan, the volcanic action has been marked which lies beyond the south eastern Bundelkhand. According to Oldham (1913) The Upper Vindhyan range consists of three main series :

(a) Bhander series,

(b) Rewah series

(c) Kaimur series.

Further, these series have been classified by him in detail into sandstones, shales and limestones.

Bundelkhand is girdled by the Vindhyan system except in the north. It starts from the Seondha Tehsil (Datia) north-west and ends in the east near Mau Tahsil, (Chitrakut) covering an area of Lalitpur, Bijawar, Ajaigarh and Kalinjar hills. The Kaimur series covers a little southern portion of Lalitpur plateau, middle part of Bijawar series and large part of Panna Tahsil. In the south of Kaimur series a narrow belt of Rewa series runs parallel. In these sand stones, a few fossils are observed which show the limit of the Upper Vindhyan system up to the lower cambrian period. Bhander series is the lower part of the Vindhyan sediments which is well marked in the west from Jabalpur to Maihar, a distance of about 200 kms.

Economically the Vindhyan sandstones are important. Besides the gems, that Vindhyan sand stones have yielded finest building stone which have been used in the construction of historic monuments.

### 3. The Alluvial Plain

The Bundelkhand plain or trans-Yamuna plain is a sub-part of 'Ganga-Yamuna Plain'. The average height from the level is between 122 to 229 metres. It is composed of alluvial deposits. Its thickness increases from the south to the north. The slope of plane follows the general slope of the region from south-west to north-east. It is well drained and well irrigated and forms fertile agricultural part of Bundelkhand. The Jalaun plain is considerably important for agricultural developments, dense population and fair distribution of settlements due to the development of Kuthond and Hamirpur branches of Betwa canal. The rail transportation also contributes a lion share in its development. The Hamirpur plain is the black soils region where agriculture is being practised without irrigation. The Turi Basin is highly fertile for Rabi crops while Maudaha Laundi tract is important for historic-culture and Betel-culture. The Rath tract is largely depends upon (Dhasan) canal irrigation, however, Laundi (Chhatarpur) tahsil is well known for the production of jowar and bajara on the black soils.

The Banda plain consists of Banda, Baberu and Naraini tehsils and is greatly significant for the double crops production. Rice-culture is being practised is this tract. Rice and Jowar, Bajara dominate among the kharif crops, whereas wheat-gram in rabi crops. This is one of the predominant agriculture region of Bundelkhand in which clustered type of settlements is universally found all rail roads and roads are main arteries of transportation.

# 4

# Drainage

That the depth of water table varies from 6 to 25 meters according to the nature of terrain. In the canal irrigated areas the water table is much above the surface due to high percentage of humidity. On the Vindhyan highland it varies on the basis of the nature of rocks. In the crystalline rocks water table is high due to less porosity and high percentage of evaporation, for example, Patha area of Chitrakoot district and Lalitpur plateau.

Numerable perennial and seasonal springs at Ajaigarh, Bijawar, Lalitpur and Karwi areas indicate the movement and direction of underground water which has least importance in the economy of the region.

The Perennial streams are great source of surface water. Fig. shows that the Yamuna is the main system of drainage which originates from the snow fed areas. Other sub-systems are the Betwa, the Dhasan, the Ken, the Sindh and the Pahuj. They are the main tributaries of the same system. They swell up in the rainy season and quickly subside into narrow deep streams. The number of seasonal torrents criss-

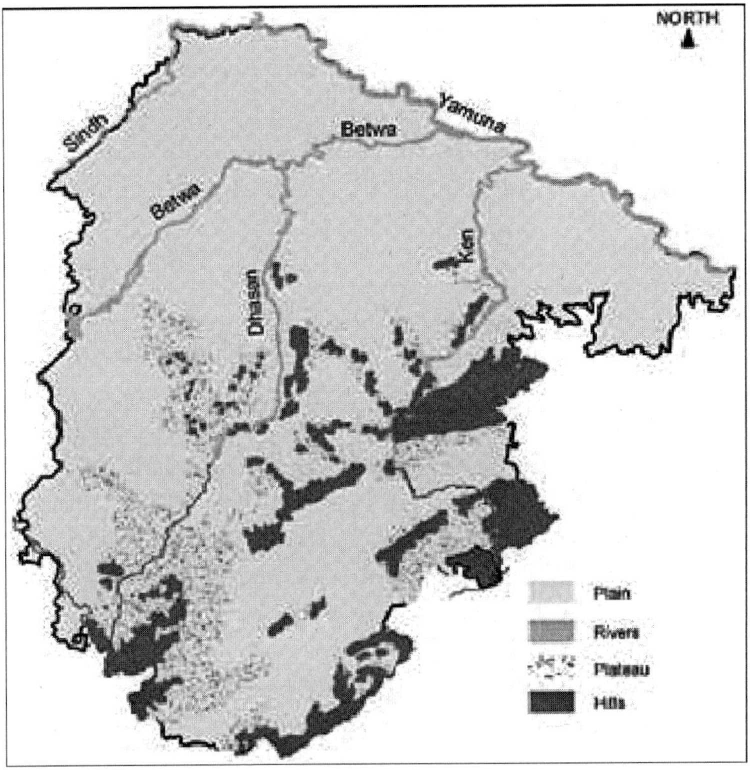


cross the land and make the surface rough and undulating. Floods often play a havoc with the life and property of the region.

### 1. The Ken

In maturity the Ken touches the region forming the district boundaries between Chhatarpur and Panna. In the upper courses it flows through the undulating hilly tracts. It is perennial stream but not navigable due to rocky beds. After leaving the M.P. State boundary aside, the Ken becomes beneficial to Banda district, supplying with sufficient water for the Ken canals. Right banks are steep and seared with ravines while the left banks are gentle and marked with alluvial deposits. Extensive alluvial plains which are called

'Tari' or 'Tir' and 'Kachhar' lower and upper beds respectively are sufficiently fertile. In rainy season it causes floods and affects the lives.

The Chandrawal is a large affluent of the Ken. Other main tributaries are Shaima, El, Bicho and Gawain.

### 2. The Betwa

It rises from the Vindhyas near the Kumri (Bhopal). After flowing 48 kms. in the south it constitutes the inter-provincial boundary between U.P. and M.P. On the upland of Bundelkhand the Betwa flows through and deep rocky beds. Near Deogarh fort it makes a magnificent sweep and cliffs. When it flows onward through the beeting banks it is scored by innumerable ravines. In some places stream fringes strip off alluvial land between the river and the cliffs. Matatila, Dhukwan and Parichha weirs are the beautiful gifts of the same which are the source of Betwa canals. Economically, the Betwa is very important among all the regional streams inspite of rocky basement. It covers largest catchment area of 21222 kms. in Bundelkhand. The Dhasan is an important tributary of the Betwa and water is drained to the Dhasan canals.

### 3. The Sindh and The Pahuj

The eastern slope of the Aravalli range is the source of the Sindh. When it marches further Nun, Parvati, Chachhond 'nalas' pour their water, as a result its carrying capacity is exceeded. Economically its valley preserves a few mineral deposits at Seondha Tahsil, where it flows cutting the Gwalior series, and melts the Yamuna near Jagammanpur.

The Pahuj is another Tributary of the Yamuna which follows the undulating course in upper part but in lower part it forms a plane. The Pahuj reservoir is a beautiful gift of the river which commands a large area for irrigation

In the eastern part of the Bagain and the Paisuni are

the main streams of Bundelkhand. Mythologically the Paisuni or the Mandakini is more important due to Ram's exile. Economically both the little rivers are insignificant.

**4. The Yamuna**

After flowing about 720 kms. in the north the river touches Bundelkhand boundary near Jagammanpur (Jalaun) where five Vindhyan streams pour their water. The Yamuna is the only river which originates from the Yamunotri 13 kms. from Kusauli (Kasol). So far its value is conserved, it is insignificant for the region because its right banks stand just like a straight high wall (20 to 60 meters) which do not permit successive penetration. However, it covers and area of 696 kms. from Agra to Mau (Chitrakut) which has historical importance.

Its rugged and high banks are unfit for irrigation and agricultural uses. The total catchment area in Bundelkhand is 9650 Sq. kms.

Bundelkhand is the region of tanks, lakes and reservoirs. Every rural and urban settlement possesses a water body. Some of them are fine large pieces of water. Majority belongs Chandela and Bundela periods barring a few of them. The main surface water bodies are Belatal, Madam Sagar, Pratap Sagar, Baruwa Sagar, Barwar lake, Machhagawan Tal, Magarwara, Pachwara, Kachreh, Goratal, Siaori lake, Ranipur Sagar, Manikpur tal and so on.

Both the state governments have constructed the numerous irrigational projects for water supply. The main are as follows: Mata-Tila Dam, Dukwan Dam, Gangau Dam, Pahuj reservoir, Lalitpur Dam, Saprar Kabrai Dam, Rangwan Dam, Arjun Dam, Ohan Dam, Jamini Dam, Nandanwara, Beniganj and others. Among Them a few water treasures are very wide and extensive in area as table 35 shows. Thus it can be concluded that there is no acute shortage of water in the region. But problem that is faced is the high rate of run off and high percentage of evaporation which the region suffers due to the sloppy terrain and extensive as well as shallow water bodies. These phenomenon cause the shortage of water in dry season. A complete overhauling of the shallow water bodies is required to undo the process.

# 5

# Climate

Climate of Bundelkhand, as in case of any other region, is largely governed by its geographical position. The harsh and dry climate of the region, no doubt, is the result of its rocky nature and scanty vegetation. The transitional location of Bundelkhand between the Ganga plain and the Vindhyas determines its sub-tropical monsoon rhythm. The Latitudinal extension of the Vindhyans retards the force of south-west (Arabian Sea branch) monsoon current. However, with the combination of the Bay of Bengal monsoon current, it causes rather heavy rainfall in the south-east part and les in the north-west part of the region.

During the winter season, dynamic sub-tropical type of anticyclones develop in the region which weaken the depressions along the front in Northern India and provide a modest amount of winter rainfall. Such atmospheric changes are totally dependent on the local disturbances.

The effects of climate are conspicuous on the regional thorny and stunted vegetal cover. Dobby (1962) has aptly remarked that 'stretches in the north of the Vindhyan land by surviving and browsing cattle and goats. The unequal distribution of precipitation effectiveness is not only to be seen on the physiological phenomenon but the prolonged drought and annual rate of evaporation which also intensely affect the socio-economic conditions.

## Temperature

There are marked temperature variations both seasonally as well as regionally. It ranges from the lowest 02.5$^0$c in January to a highest 50.8$^0$cm in May and varies from south-east to north-west with an annual amplitude of about 24$^0$c. Hot season prolongs for about eight months when the mean monthly temperature remains high about 22.3$^0$c (Table-2). During summer the absolute maximum diurnal temperature shoots up to 47$^0$c (e.g. Jhansi : May 47.2$^0$c (2019), 48.3$^0$c (2020), and Panna : May 48.3$^0$c (2019). But the minimum diurnal temperature in the winter months seldom goes below zero centigrade (for instance Jhansi : February 0$^0$c (2020) and December 3.3$^0$c (2020), Nowgaon : December 0$^0$c (2020) and January 1.66$^0$c (2020) and Panna : January 6$^0$c (2020).

Besides the above examples in 2020 about 3498 and 108 villages respectively of Jhansi, Jalaun,

**Table - 2**

**Temperature (in C) 2020**

| Month | Jhansi | Nowgaon | Banda |
|---|---|---|---|
| January | 19.2 | 15.6 | 23.7 |
| February | 20.2 | 13.8 | 27.9 |
| March | 22.8 | 24.6 | 34.1 |
| April | 31.8 | 32.5 | 39.5 |
| May | 48.5 | 46.5 | 43.0 |
| June | 49.6 | 47.8 | 40.8 |

| July | 32.5 | 31.6 | 34.0 |
|---|---|---|---|
| August | 27.4 | 27.4 | 32.1 |
| September | 26.6 | 27.2 | 33.1 |
| October | 21.9 | 27.5 | 32.1 |
| November | 21.5 | 26.8 | 29.2 |
| December | 14.5 | 24.7 | 14.2 |

## Rainfall

Monsoon plays ducks and drakes with the regional economy. A good monsoon means a prosperous year and vice-versa. As the variability of rainfall, both seasonal and micro-regional is great, it has far reaching effects on its agrarian economy. Rainfall is caused by both the Arabian Sea current and the Bay of Bengal current, the latter having the upper hand. However, their influence is weak. But wherever the two currents interact, heavy rain is caused. G.C. Sympton has laid stress on this feature, that the cooling is a major cause of the heavy rains and the local distribution of rainfall being determined by the position of the ranges in relation to the wind direction.

### Table - 3

### Rainfall (in cm.) year - 2020

| Stations | Jan | Feb. | Mar. | Apr. | May | June | July | Aug. | Sept. | Oct. | Nov. | Dec. |
|---|---|---|---|---|---|---|---|---|---|---|---|---|
| Lalitpur | 02 | – | – | 01 | – | 47 | 165 | 109 | 118 | 28 | – | 04 |
| Jhansi | 03 | 05 | – | 03 | – | 134 | 141 | 139 | 110 | 18 | – | 05 |
| Jalaun | 01 | 02 | – | 02 | – | 15 | 195 | 135 | 135 | 22 | – | 03 |
| Hamirpur | 02 | 01 | – | 01 | – | 16 | 197 | 146 | 127 | 21 | – | 06 |
| Mahoba | 02 | – | – | 01 | – | 42 | 165 | 107 | 116 | 29 | – | 02 |
| Banda | 01 | 02 | – | 02 | – | 49 | 155 | 146 | 48 | 70 | – | 05 |
| Chitrakoot | 01 | 02 | – | 01 | – | 48.25 | 154.5 | 142 | 47.5 | 6.5 | – | 06 |
| Datia | 02 | 04 | – | 02 | – | 135 | 143 | 127 | 114 | 16 | – | 04 |
| Tikamgarh | 02 | – | – | 01 | – | 125 | 168 | 109 | 120 | 27 | – | 03 |
| Chhatarpur | 03 | 03 | – | 02 | – | 175 | 186 | 198 | 168 | 12 | – | 06 |

| | | | | | | | | | | | | |
|---|---|---|---|---|---|---|---|---|---|---|---|---|
| Panna | 02 | 04 | - | 03 | - | 215 | 222 | 229 | 212 | 18 | - | 04 |
| Sagar | 02 | 04 | - | 01 | - | 234 | 241 | 236 | 245 | 17 | - | 07 |
| Damoh | 03 | 02 | - | 02 | - | 195 | 186 | 175 | 136 | 15 | - | 06 |
| Niwari | 01 | 02 | - | 01 | - | 129 | 175 | 97 | 117 | 23 | 02 | 03 |
| Gwalior | 03 | 01 | 01 | 02 | - | 192 | 168 | 227 | 235 | 15 | - | 04 |
| Satna | 02 | 02 | - | - | - | 205 | 186 | 129 | 136 | 21 | 03 | 06 |

The following characteristics of the regional rainfall are noticeable :-

(1) The beginning of rains may be delayed or They may occur very early.

(2) The monsoon may cease prematurely before usual dates.

(3) The prolonged breaks may punctuate the rainy season.

(4) The rain may be heavy and persist for a longer period.

(5) Irregular warm and dry air blows from the north-west, interrups the monsoon rains completely.

(6) The sub-tropical cyclone are the other causes of areal differenciations.

(7) Relief is the other factor which adds to the complexities.

## Climatic Regions

A great variety of elements from east to west have been noted in the classification of the regional climatic types. Koppen's, Thornthwaite's, Kendrew and Stamp's classification of climate are more familiar and noteworthy. But these are not enough to classify a particular sub-division, having many shortcomings in general. Mostly temperature and precipitation have been taken into consideration as the main element in classifying the climate, while a particular wind, air mass or pressure system should also be taken into account for a genetic classification. Thornthwaite has divided a great part of India within CA'w type of climate when much diversity is found in each climatic factor from east to west and south to north. Broadly speaking Koppen's classification follows the natural limit of the Vindhyan land and divided into 'AW' (Tropical Savannah) and 'CWg' (Gangetic or continental). According to his arid and semi arid formula 'Aw' climate must be designated as 'Aw' in the region. Because south eastern part of Bundelkhand is more humid than the north western part. It will be more suitable to denote the north-west portion of the region in 'BSH' type in place of 'CWg' due to the nearness of arid region of Rajputana.

## Seasonal Patterns

### 1. October to December

The rains assisting in premature stage causes greater harm than delayed rain. Due to this fact water scarcity is experienced for rabi crops which dry up according to the agriculture calender. After September the temperature gradually cools down filling the nights because the belt of low pressure is transferred towards the east and retreating monsoon current curves round, occasional showers are caused from east to west. The sky remains cloudless most of the season and humidity slackness considerably down by degrees till November but again resumes it upward trend in early December. "The rice harvest is gathered and the threshing is done in pleasant condition, fields to be sown with wheat or barley are ploughed..." during this season.

### 2. January to March

After October the atmosphere pressure begins to intensify over the whole region due to south-ward march of the sun. Gradually atmosphere cools down and December and January are considered to be the coldest months of the season. The mean monthly temperature varies between 13.1$^0$C and 12.2$^0$C and sometimes temperature goes down below the zero centigrade and causes severe frost as mentioned previously. Humidity is quite low and sky almost cloudless over most of the region. Sometimes western disturbances which are the continuation of 'Mediterranean Depression' travel eastwards across the northern India and cause cloudy weather and appreciable rains in the month of January. The rabi crops of northern and central India are benefited immensely from timely winter rains. As a whole cold weather is a pleasant season for the well clad, well fed and well housed.

### 3. April to June

In Bundelkhand hot weather is much less pleasant and more unhealthy than winter due to the exceedingly high temperature. It being somewhat earlier and last a longer period than in the Ganga-Yamuna Doab dominated by local weather conditions. When the sun crawls towards the tropics the atmospheric currents go on changing and pressure falls rapidly with the rising temperature after the elapse of the month of February. The westerlies disturb the tranquility of the atmosphere and influence the standing rabi crops which are generally ready for the sickle before the maturity in the beginning of the month of March. The air moisture decreases and temperature rises rapidly in the months of May and Jund. Both the months are the hotest months of the year rendering an average temperature of 34.4$^0$C and often reaches about 48$^0$C. The nights of Bundelkhand are soothing and pleasand because of the rocky nature of its topography.

The winds from west are more effective at the end of March, blowing 'strongly' in April and May and lasting with frequent intermissions of easterly breeze till early June. Dust-storms (andhi) are very strong in the north-west part and their force diminishes towards the east. In the east dust winds have two special characteristics purity and transparency in the air. Because Mar and Kabar soils give off a little dust particles. In such purifies atmosphere the sun directly strikes the earth's surface. These strong winds bring a sudden change in atmosphere and causes bad effects. In May scorching hot wind (Loo) blow uninterrupted till the filling of the sunset, carrying with the low percentage of (about 6%) humidity. The severity of the heat and exposure of the sunny blaze are dangerous to the lives.

### 4. July to September

Hot weather ends just followed by rainy season. The south-west monsoon is the main current of regional meteorology. First shower starts after the second week of June but sometime fluctuates later or sooner. Uncertainty prevails and chance plays a a significant role in this regard. The maximum temperature of June creates 'the monsoon though of low pressure in the north-west part of the country. The quantity of rainfall totally depends on the cyclonic storms and depressions which help to bring about an equitable distribution of rainfall in the interior of the sub-continent. July and August are the rainiest months of the year which is evident by Table-4. About 90 percent rainfall and 75 percent rainy days are concentrated within three months of the year.

# 6

# Soils

Soils of every region reflect its geomorphic history and some areas do so better than do the land forms. Bundelkhand demonstrates the validity of the above statement and the soil types faithfully reflect the nature of terrain. Geologically speaking, soils of the region are entirely different from the Ganga-Yamuna doab. The soils range from mature rich black cotton soils to immature residual stoney soils.

Soils derive their characteristics from the parental materials, and some of the beds are highly ferruginous and have iron pockets due to lateritic actions. The pedologists classify soils 'its fertility-status for crop production, its probable reaction to rainfall or irrigation and its response to treatments cultural and manurial'.

**Bundelkhand Soils**

| 1 | 2 | 3 | 4 |
|---|---|---|---|
| / | / | / | / |
| Upland Soils | Lowland Soils | Riverine Soils | Local Soils |
| 1. Stoney soils | / | 1. Kachhar | 1. Goind |

2. Forest Soils Black Soil 2. Tari 2. Kherwa
Red & Yellow
/ Soils. 3. Gaurihar
/ / 4. Dandi
1. Mar (Mawa) 1. Parua 5. Satwari etc

## Table -4

## Classification of Soils and their Characteristics (2020)

| Description | Type I | | Type II | | Type III | |
|---|---|---|---|---|---|---|
| | IA | IB | IIA | IIB | IIIA | IIIB |
| | Soil of rocky ridges | Coarse grained reddish soil | Brownish loam soils | Gray loan soils | Coarse grained black soil | Clayey black soil |
| Profile development | Not described agricultural unimportant | Immature | Mature | Mature | Mature | Mature |
| Colour | - | Reddish | Brownish | Light gray to dark gray | Dark gray to black | Black |
| Concretions | - | Absent | Kankarbed | Kankarbed | Slight | Kankar |
| Texture | - | Sandy | Loam | Sandy-10am | Clay loam | Clayey |
| Lime | - | 1.0 % | Low at surface & high at bottom | Low at surface and high at bottom | About 1.0% throughout | 1.5% |
| pH | - | 7-8 | 7.5 - 8.5 | 7.5 - 8.5 | 7 - 8 | 7 - 8 |
| Magmesoa | - | Equal to lime % | Less the lime % | Less than lime % | Less than lime % | Less than lime % |
| Clay | - | 6.3 % | 13 to 45 % | 13 - 45 % | 20 - 50 % | 40 - 50 % |
| Coarse sand | - | 17 - 70% | 2 - 7 % | 6 - 38 % | 4 - 11 % | 1 - 2 % |
| Soluble salts | - | Low | Low | Low | Low | Low |
| Drainage | - | Excessive | Good | Good | Poor | Poor |
| Nature | - | Unproductive | Less productive | Moderate in Fertility | Medium to high in Fertility | High fertility |

These soils cover extreme south elevated areas, at hill foot fans and slopes especially on the Patha tract of (Chitrakoot) and Lalitpur Plateau. In these areas the soil removal proportion is greater than soil formation due to high erosion by water agency. Locally these are called in various names such as, Pathari on Lalitpur plateau; 'Bhota' or 'Situhari' on Path Tract. These are easily permeable by air and water to aerate the plant roots but often suffer from severe droughts. Because in these areas the percentage of run-off and evaporation is greater than water availability. The hills and hillocks covered with considerable vegetation in some places contain fertile soils with greater quantity of humus. Forest soils are deposited by weathering agencies in the shallow areas of the rocky tracts. As compared to sandy soils of Type I, they have greater productive capacity. But the prospects of agriculture are limited due to shallowness and hardness. In Lalitpur district forest soils are called 'Dand' (jungle) which are composed of iron oxide accumulation alkaline, earth metals and the mobility of silica sand marks the red colour of the soil.

## Soil Erosion and Conservation

The problem of soil erosion is serious one in the case of Type I and II and it is much more serious along the river courses of the Yamuna, the Betwa, the Ken, the Dhasan, the Pahuj, and the Sindh. Where the erosional land-scape is seen in the panorama of 'Bihad' (bad land) forms. Universally the region suffers sheet erosion on the cultivated areas, by which the top fertile layer of the soil is eroded gradually in a mass-que. Texture of soil, vegetal cover, intensity of rainfall and slope of the landscape all are responsible for that. Such faulty practices as ploughing through the contours of unbounded fields hasten both gully and sheet erosion. In recent years unplanned felling and thinning of the vegetal cover, uncontrolled grazing and failure to replant trees have led to forest erosion of alarming proportions. The entire area beyond the north of the Vindhyan ridges is badly affected.

More than one-third are of the region comes under the

red washable character of soils. And major portion of the region is either free from dense vegetal cover or it has poor vegetation which do not check the soil erosion perfectly. The farmers have also aggravated this problem, because either they are unaware of the improved methods of agricultural farming or are not taking interest in the new techniques. They are engaged in removing the forest and have utilized all the pasture lands for agricultural purpose. Therefore, the water flows unhindered.

More than half of the cultivated area in Bundelkhand is in urgent need of erosion control primarily by contour bunding, and also by such methods as contour ploughing and trenching and strip cropping. Soil work not only maintains the soil fertility and productivity but also prevents further deterioration of land. It can also be restored by other means such as crop rotations, irrigation, afforestation, prohibition of overgrazing. The necessary earth moving may be done by machines such as bulldozers. Improved methods of agriculture can be utilised as U.S.A and Japan have done to control this growing problem.

**Table - 5**

**Soil Conservation : (In three successive Five Year Plan in Rupees (000)**

| District | Achievement in IX Five year plan (1997-2002) | Achievement in XII Five year plan (2012-2017) | Total proposed Target (2017-2022) |
|---|---|---|---|
| **Lalitpur** | 32,547 | 35,958 | 37,095 |
| **Jhansi** | 39,890 | 45,140 | 48,890 |
| **Jalaun** | 33,282 | 36,693 | 37,830 |
| **Hamirpur** | 23,526 | 26,937 | 28,074 |

| Mahoba | 15,842 | 19,253 | 20,390 |
|---|---|---|---|
| Banda | 26,801 | 30,212 | 31,349 |
| Chitrakoot | 25,323 | 28,734 | 29,871 |
| Datia | 27,685 | 31,096 | 32,233 |
| Tikamgarh | 24,175 | 27,586 | 28,723 |
| Chhatarpur | 35,360 | 38,771 | 39,908 |
| Panna | 15,135 | 18,546 | 19,683 |
| Sagar | 33,255 | 36,666 | 37,803 |
| Damoh | 31,365 | 34,776 | 35,913 |
| Niwari | - | - | 21,264 |
| Gwalior | 27,165 | 36,565 | 32,335 |
| Satna | 31,465 | 33,436 | 34,474 |

# 7

# Minerals

## Gypsum

There are three important gypsum deposits, located on the alluvial plain. Two of them Puraini and Katihar villages lie to the west and east respectively of the Barma river a tributary of Betwa in Rath Tahsil (Hamirpur). The Ore is confined within an area of about 350 meters in this locality and its thickness is about 60 cm. In the south of Puraini village there is an area of about 60 cm. In the south of Puraini village there is an area of about 225 meters where the mineral can be mined. 'Sarila' village is the third centre in the same district where it is available.

## Iron-Ore

Bijawar and Gwalior series of Bundelkhand have some 'pockets of iron-ore at variable heights'. There are two important iron-ore centres located at Moti and Devar in Bijawar series which are about 24 kms. only, to the east of the Bijawar town. During the period of the Bundela Chiefs the Motee iron mines supplied ores for making swords and other war materials.

'Par Hill' of Gwalior series is also rich in iron-ore reserve. 'Sold' and 'Sonrai' mines near Jhansi district, have local importance. Munchh-Bhoti iron-mines are located in the Vindhyachal range, in the north of Panna district. Geological Survey Department has reported a mass of iron-ore near Manikpur in the Kalyangarh Pargana. It was famous for the fine quality of iron ore in the same pargana at Gobarahi village.

Although Bundelkhand possesses iron-ore deposits its quality of haematite is not superior so as to compete in the market. Moreover, there is leaching defect and problem of transportation.

## Pyrophyllite

It is useful industrial mineral and occurs in Hamirpur, Jhansi and Tikamgarh districts with sufficient deposits. Estimated deposits at Gorahiri and Bijri are about 2,30,000 and 5,66,000 tons respectively.

After testing its utility, a refractory plant is planned at Lalitpur which will carry a capacity of 62,000 metric tons to be reached.

## Bauxite

A vast range of bauxite deposits has recently been reported by the 'Geological Programming Board' between the Allahabad and Chitrakoot districts. The reserve is estimated around the 10 million metric tones. It has been proved by these huge deposits that a great scope of a big aluminium plant exists in the region. Actually the state government is not paying proper attention to develop this costly mineral, else its development would bring economic prosperity to the region as well as to the state. It will also give work a large number of unemployed persons.

## Diamond

Volcanic pipe at Majhgawan; it is situated 22 kms. south-west of Panna and covers and area of 500 meters. It is based on the result of an exploratory bore hole drilled by the Geological Survey of India to a depth of 100 meters. The country rocks around the pipe an almost horizontally bedded quartzite Sand stone of the Kaimur range. Alluvial deposits at Ram Kheria : it is situated 32 kms. south-west of Panna and covers an area of about 10 sq.km. The estimated reserves is 1,15,000 emirates. Diamondiferous Conglomerate which extend all along the belt. The area. from Chhatarpur to Kalinjar has been known to be diamond ferous. The belt is about 96 kms. long and about 16 kms. wide. According to Vredenburg the principal diamond bearing layer lies between the upper Vindhyan series and the Kaimur Sand-stones. These diamond beds of shales are locally known as 'Kakra'. Field study reveals that diamonds are also found in government occupied areas where licence holder extract the gems. A layer of the gravel exists at a depth of 2 meters. On the bank of Kilkila river near Panna. Majhgawan and Ramkheria are the two important mines which have been nationalised and the National Mineral Development Corporation (NMDC) is working. In both the places suddenly settlements grow up in the midst of dense forest, based on the mineral resources.

## Building Stones

The Bundelkhand region is very rich in building stones. Not only the present but all the historical monuments from the Mughal period to the British period attest the building utility of these Vindhyan rocks. Throughout the region, coarse and fine granite is quarried especially in adjoining districts of Chhatarpur, Tikamgarh, Hamirpur, Banda and Jhansi districts. Chanda-Pahar (Hamirpur) Kabrai (Mahoba), Shivrampur (Chitrakoot) and Jhansi city are the main centres of this industry. The main slab quarry centres in the upper Vindhyans are Dhurra, Jakhlone, Narhat (Lalitpur), Dargawan (Chattarpur) and near Karwi and Manikpur

(Chitrakoot). The slabs are extensively used for roofing purposes in the indigenous houses of Bundelkhand. Sand stone and lime stone are the chief raw building materials of the Vindhyan mountains. The upper layer of Bhander range contains pink variety of sand stones. Their texture is uniform and soft which is useful for the construction of the buildings, dams and bridges. It is transported to the neighbouring urban centres. Limestone appears on the top of the Semri or lower Vindhyan beds of the Bundelkhand. The sand is an important building material in modern age. Bundelkhand sand is famous for its fine quality that is known as red-gold. The regional rivers stores it and supply to the rural and urban centers abundantly.

### Clay

The fine grained quality of clay is found on the northern plain of the region. It has local importance for tile and wall making and for the purpose of plastering houses. It is also widely used for brick making. The China clay is available in Chhatarpur district in a huge quantity, which can be utilized to make the glass dolls. Fire clay is very useful for brick making industry.

### Sillica Sand

It is worked out near Bargarh village on the border of Chitrakoot and Allahabad districts. Quartz and granitic and stone of Rajgarh have also some commercial importance. So far as the production is concerned, it has no economic value. But production can be increased on the basis of favourable conditions. The production of silica sand in U.P. is expected to rise to a level of 2.0 million tons. It is estimated that the reserves of the same belt are as 100 million metric tons approximately. Further attempts are being made to extend the area as well as the production through Dhabansa, Panhai and Manikpur to Jhansi district.

## Ochres

A huge mass of ochre deposits exist in the south-west of Lakhanpur village in Karwi Tahsil of Chitrakoot district. Here red and yellow colour ochre are found along with the white clay. The reserves are estimated to be about 10-15 thousand metric tons. The other important area is located in the Seondha tehsil of Datia district. The third important ochre centre exists near Jamunia in Panna district. The production of Ochre in 2020 reached 405.22 metric tons. Looking at huge reserve of Ochres, a good deal can be said about the future prospects of Paint and Varnish industry in the region.

# 8

# Natural Vegetation

The vegetal cover of the landscape is the product of its physiographic, climatic, edaphic and biotic conditions. In Bundelkhand natural vegetation passes into transitional type, which is characterised by a smaller number of species, diminishing density and is particularly marked by periodicity in leaf-shedding. The intensity of rainfall and soil characteristics determine the character of vegetation. As rainfall increases toward south and south-east, the forest (during the wet season) may show a density and luxuriance analogous to that of the rain forest. Comparatively, the woods are not so thick, lines not developed on the same scale, and the trees do not reach quite the same height. 'The theoretical distinction between the luxuriant monsoonal forest and true rain forest is that the former includes a considerable proportion of trees which shed their leaves during the dry season e.g., Teak (Tectona-grandis)'. The eroded and poor soils contain less moisture, stunted shrubs and thorny forests and are more scattered in favourable localities such as near water sources. "The level grounds in between the low lying grounds and the cultivated fields are generally occupied by meadow vegetation open to grazaing".

On the basis of administrative set up the forests have been divided into three main types:

### 1. Reserved Forests

These are property of the government. The percentage of reserved forest is high in Chhatarpur (72.54), first and Panna (43.00) and Sagar (42.00) follows the same.

### 2. Protected Forests

The trees of these forests belong to the government but land is occupied by the people. The licence is issued to cut the trees and to graze the cattle. Chhatarpur (47.45), Panna (46.00) and Sagar (45.00) have high percentage protected forests.

### 3. Unclassed or Open Forests

These forests are owned by the big landlords. Economically these are not much significant. The percentage of unclassed forest area is high in Hamirpur, Mahoba, Jalaun and Lalitpur districts.

**Table - 6**

**Administrative Classification of Forests (%) Year - 2020**

| District | Reserved | Protected | Unclassed |
|---|---|---|---|
| **Lalitpur** | 14.55 | - | 85.55 |
| **Jhansi** | 47.69 | 0.89 | 51.42 |
| **Jalaun** | 13.43 | - | 86.57 |
| **Hamirpur** | 4.00 | - | 96.00 |
| **Mahoba** | 5.50 | 1.46 | 93.04 |
| **Banda** | 32.56 | - | 67.44 |

| Chitrakoot | 36.50 | 1.36 | 62.14 |
|---|---|---|---|
| Datia | 61.58 | 38.42 | - |
| Tikamgarh | - | 100 | - |
| Chhatarpur | 72.54 | 21.20 | 6.26 |
| Panna | - | 100 | - |
| Sagar | 50.15 | 0.95 | 48.90 |
| Damoh | 44.15 | 0.85 | 55.00 |
| Niwari | - | 100 | - |
| Gwalior | 51.2 | 0.75 | 48.05 |
| Satna | 42.25 | 0.65 | 57.10 |

## Conservation of Forests

'Dhaiya' or shifting cultivation heavily depleted the canopy from the pre-historic period. Increasing the needs of wood and timber during peace and war times have directly affected the tree crops. The villagers slipped and felled the trees for fodder and firewood and the forests were over-grazed by herbs and flocks. High growth rate of population for last five decades required more land for agriculture, settlement and communication lines. Hence pressure of population on cultivated land led to deforestation for 'Navtor' (breaking of virgin soil). The rights of grazing, lopping and collecting all sorts of minor products are contested among various claimants and cutting of timber for fuel woods excessively, open the natural cover which the land once luxuriantly forested, and are now becoming mere scrubby waste. This has resulted in the acceleration of erosion, inking the water table, sedimentation in streams, devastation of floods. People must be made to understand that misuse and destruction of the forest wealth gives the protection to soil, water resources and climate. The trees adorn the homes, cities, towns and village.

The conservation of 'green gold' and the wild life is not only the duty of a few officials but also every member of the society. 'Forest fire problem' is serious one. It cannot be completely controlled without the co-operation of the public because the experience of forest authorities says that the forest fire is mostly man made. Adequate protection measures should be taken. The fire-fighting equipments can be operated. It is reported that the forest departments of the Bundelkhand region have no equipment which can be quickly pressed into service. The village forest societies should be introduced for better management of the forests.

The government should provide training for protecting the forest wealth. Forest dispensary is also needed in the region which can control the insects and diseases. Fungal diseases have made serious on road on the forest resources. Over grazing on the waste land should be checked and such areas may be encouraged for afforestation. deforested land will be-able to provide timber, fuel, fodder, new grazing lands, beautiful landscapes, pleasant sylvan retreats and recreational grounds, because 'forests precede civilization but desert succeed them'. The State Governments have realised the urgent need to create fuel and fodder reserves. Working plans for the management of canal plantations have been revised to increase the production of firewood. Roadside avenues, railway station yards, camping grounds and other culturable waste lands have been utilized for the supplementing the supplies of fuel, fodder and timber. It is gratifying to note that the 'Van Mahotsav Festival' is observed every year. Numbers new trees are planted by the institutions, the administrators and forest authorities.

Some useful recommendations have been in a Seminar

for the plantation in the Bundelkhand Region.

1) Original top soils abutting agricultural land are suited for Sissu, Babul, Siris and Neem.
2) Eroded domes and Kankar accumulations for prosopis juliflora.
3) Upper eroded slopes with Kankar Khair, Siris, but Neem in deeper soils.
4) Lower slopes with deeper soils - Neem, Siris and Babul (Babul in frost free locations).
5) Valley bottoms - Sissu and Bamboo (Bamboo along stream banks).

# 9

# Animal Husbandry

Bundelkhand is one of the three important zoo-geographical regions of the country which provides habitation and sustenance for numerous fauna families. The Vindhyan ranges, forests and streams have abundant food, shelter and water and provide other favourable factors for sheltering the wild lives. Up to the beginning of the present century the region was thickly forested and was very rich in wild lives too. There were good hunting grounds near Seondha (Datia), Ranipur (Chitrakoot), Ajaigarh (Panna) and Lalitpur areas. Now the jungle beasts are steadily declining because sparse vegetation is unable to sustain rich wild animals like lion, tiger and other carnivora. This is partly due to indiscriminate hunting, brutal cutting of jungles and also due to more areas having been brought under cultivation.

The Felidae or cat family includes Tiger (felis tigris), Panther (felis pardus), and wild cat (felis charges). These carnivora wild lives are widely distributed in the Panna and the Vindhyachal ranges, and the Lalitpur plateau. But owing to the extension of cultivation, the growth of population and the greater use of fire-arms they are fast diminishing in number. Of the dog family the wolf (canis lupus), the Jackal (canisaureus), the Fox, the Bherkis, the wild dog, the Boars and the Hyaena (Striata) are very common in the ravines as well as in the plains. The wolf and the hyaena take a heavy toll of sheep, goats, cattle and ponees. The carrion-eating striped hyenas is in abundance in waste lands.The species of the stage and antelope families are very common in Bundelkhand. The Sambhar (Corvus Unicolor), Chinkara (Gaze lle benetti) and Black buck (Anti lope cervicapra) are the finest species of Bundelkhand wild lives, which are found specially in the southern hills of the region. The Barking deer (Muntiacus muntjac), Nilgai (Portax pictus) and spotted deer (Axis maculatus) are quite common throughout the region while they have suffered heavy depredation in the hands of indiscriminate hunters. They are very notorious for the destruction of the cultivated fields specially near the jungles. 'The experience of cultivators suggest that greater damage to their crops is done by wild bores which raid their fields in the night'. On this accounts its killing is the commonest game near the forests. The wild pigs and monkeys greatly ravage crops near Chitrakoot hills. All sorts of common of ten birds, fishes, reptiles and microorganisms are abundantly found in the region. On the whole Bundelkhand is sufficiently rich in natural assets. The preservation of the wild life is necessary because several important species are now either extinct or on the point of extinction. The ancient sculptures of Khajuraho, Dudhari, Sagar, Datia, Kalinjar and Mahoba are proof that the early kings had much sympathy is protection of wild life. They were the lover of the natural assets. For example, the forests of Panna were protected by the 'Panna State Shikhar Rules' and in state shooting of Carnivora was permitted only to the members of ruling family. At present the following enactments extend over the forests :-

It is obvious that the region has a few fine and valuable species but there is no sanctuary to protect these mute wild animals. It can be suggested that the region requires a sanctuary where beautiful varieties of creatures can be preserved. Black-buck is one of the most beautiful species in antelope family and the only representative of its kind in the world which is becoming increasingly hard to find. Such rare variety must be protected by all means.

The protection to the flora is important from the following points of view :-

1) To maintain an equilibrium between the vegetal canopy and animal kingdoms and the animals themselves.

2) It is essential for valuable research as well as for educational and aesthetic values.

3) At the same time these are both friends and foes of the cultivators because they consume the injurious pests, insects and weeds.

4) These are a great source of food, medicine and foreign exchange.

5) Religiously, to save their life is sacred.

It is necessary to control the general shooting of wild life in those areas which are capable of providing food. It is necessary to conserve wild life in our recreational and historical places.

# Human Geography

# 10

# Houses

The House is a universal element of the cultural landscape which displays the inter-relationship between man and his habitat. Dickens has aptly remarked, houses are as varied as people and environment with which they are associated. Houston recognize it as the symbol of regionalism by which the social organisation of its inhabitants and the rural economy, both have distinct manifestation.

It will not be out of place to define the term house. According to Bryan it includes all human structures whether they are meant to live in or work in or store things in. There is no reason to doubt that the term house has very wide connotation. The aim of geographic study of houses is to analyse the form, structure and layout in response to physical, economic and social conditions. The form and structure of a house exhibit the impact of geographic conditions the availability of the building materials, architecture styles, the nature of roofing and wall, shape and direction of face and façade. The lay out of house or house-plan represents the socio-economic needs of the people and the climate characteristics.

### Factors Influencing House Types

Major factors which influence the house types are –

1. Physical Factors
2. Cultural Factors

### 1. Physical Factors

Physical factors have direct bearing upon the house construction as Nishi has remarked that region difference in the physical environment are the most readily observed correlates relating to farm-house variation. In the words of Singh, the natural environment has not only determined the nature of building materials, but also has influenced the form of roof.

### Building Materials

The building material guides the hand of the architect and the peculiarities of form and structure follow therefrom. People generally use those building materials which are cheap and readily available in the close vicinity.

### Climate

Truly speaking, the house protects against the climatic elements. Hence the shape, size, orientation are greatly determined by their regional differentiation. Brunhes remarks that climate expresses itself through the form of roof. Insolation and temperature, amount of rainfall, wind direction and wind velocity are the major climatic elements which have influenced the house types of Bundelkhand.

### Insolation and Temperature

The impact of high temperature is reflected in the construction of regional house types. In hot weather large gable roof with good air space provides more comfortable atmosphere to the dwellers. Actually, the courtyard, gallery, windows and verandahs are other adjustments to temperature conditions.

### Rainfall

The amount of rainfall widely influences the external form the house through the areal variation. From the south-east to the north-west peculiar variation of rainfall have been noted already in the chapter on climate, that the quantity of rainfall is high in the fringe of the Vindhyans exhibits.

### Winds

The direction of the prevailing winds play a significant role in designing the shape and face of the regional houses. In Bundelkhand, westerlies blow about nine-ten months in a year. The people make use of broad gables fixed towards wind direction. It is also remarkable that people do not prefer to orient their houses towards the west in order to escape the sand and dust particles coming with westerlies. With this end in view practically all settlements of the hills and hillocks have selected leeward sites.

## 2. Cultural Factors

Generally houses of the rich and the poor vary in many respects. The poor people cannot afford the costly building materials while the well to do persons spend a lot in construction of beautiful modern houses. Economic factors affect not only the architecture of the house but also its plan.

### General Morphology

One room dwelling of the poor families are compact where men and live-stock find shelter under the same roof. They are rectangular in plan and are built of local materials. Roof is framed on both the sides with the help of ridge log in the centre. Houses with two-rooms are often L-shaped and houses with three rooms are U-shaped surrounded by wall from one side. Bakhari is centrally located so that further extension may be made conveniently. More than four room dwellings belong to join families and are multifunctional.

In Bundelkhand economic factor governs the social factor because the regional Muslim population is mostly converted Hindus of Mughal times so that there is, but a slight, difference in the shape and size of houses of the two communities. In a Muslim house there is a separate apartment for females. The tribal habitations like those of the Kols, the Sahariya, the Sonar and the Khairwar are totally different from a multiple dwelling of a joint Hindu family. Houston has rightly remarked that social factors are apparent in the tribal organization and religious features of certain house types.

## Morphology of the Dwellings

In the analysis of the house morphology all the physical and cultural factors are involved which have caused the regional and cultural variations in building materials, house plans, shapes and sizes of the houses. Floor plan also reflects the standard of living and occupational characteristics of the dwellers. Plans do differ between agricultural (the Lodhi, the Kurmi, the Ahir) and non-agricultural communities (shop keeper, Lohar, Darji, Chamar, Sonar, etc).

## Common Features of the Dwellings

The most common features of the rural dwelling in bundelkhand is Bakhari or Angan (open courtyard). A square or rectangular open space surrounded by rooms on all four sides, or on two or three sides and the remaining side is enclosed by walls as shown.

## Classification of House Types and Their Regional Distribution

The French and German scholars have classified house

types into two primary divisions – (1) the single compact dwelling (maison bloc or en heithaus) and (2) the multiple dwellings (maison-cour of gehoft).

This classification is purely based on the plan of the house rather than the physical and cultural factors. The house pattern, use of social space and building materials reflect the condition of rural economy, population density, settlement pattern and standard of living.

To differentiate the rural dwellings, it is necessary to consider the nature of building materials according to the natural environment and economic and social conditions of the people. The Bundelkhand dwellings can be well classified on the basis of :

(a) Socio-cultural variation

(b) Size and shape variation

(c) The building material variation

## The Thatched House

Rudimentary thatched hut is the symbol of rural India. In Bundelkhand mainly the tribal people erect such typical shelter. It is, doubtless, that these are the traits of their backwardness, migratory and temporary existence. Such structures are unsafe, unhygienic and ugly in look. In special distribution they are sprinkled near the jungles where the thatching grasses or 'kharas' are predominantly available.

## Stone House

The stone house is the symbol of durability and prosperity. Masonry buildings forts and fortresses at Khajuraho, Deogarh, Mahoba, Kalinjar and Jhansi still display their grandeur. Most of them are located near the stone quarry centres on the Vindhyan land. It serves both the purpose, as roof and wall material. Besides stone, other building materials like wood and mud are also available nearby. But people prefer stone due to its durable quality, near the quarry centres.

## The Brick House

Away from high Vindhyan ranges and forest areas where stone slabs and slates and thatching grasses are not available, clay is the only building material. Clayey soil is easily converted into bricks and tiles, hence the regional people are busy in replacing the kachcha houses with Pucca brick houses. Such dwellings show the advancement of the civilization and prosperity.

## Tiled House

The mud wall and tile roof dwellings are very common especially in the alluvial plains of Bundelkhand. The tiles are made of local mud and baked with dry dung fuel. After framing by beams, poles, logs, reeds and stalks of arhar tiles are arranged systematically on the roof. Mud walls are paved with clay by mixing the rice husk or straw of paddy or wheat so that the rain shower may not erode the wall. House plan is the same as we have stated above. Residential accommodation varies according to the economic condition and social status.

## Problem

There are two different aspects of the housing problem (i) the unsatisfactory character of the existing accommodations from the view point of hygiene and public health; and (ii) shortage of housing. In single compact houses where men and livestock find shelter under the same roof, unhygienic conditions prevail. The houses of the several poor families are low, small, dark and clingy. They become so accustomed to live in these novels that sometimes they lose interest in improving the living conditions. In compact settlements where houses are built wall to wall, overcrowding and congestion mar the residential atmosphere. Houses are built without any thought planning and ventilation. Lanes are winding and some-times blind too. Social space is subjected to increasing pressure of population. There is no proper arrangement of drainage and water supply. The standard of rural dwellings is definitely lower than that of the urban areas. Not only do most of the dwellings lack modern sanitation, but also a large number of houses are defective and dilapidated. Open latrine system makes the sanitary condition still worse.

The other problem in this context is the shortage of homes. The need of more houses has been greatly experienced for the last three decades due to increase of population in both the rural and urban areas. This problem is not only acute in our country but also abroad. The changes in age distribution, the proportion of people of marrying age and settling up separate households etc. have contributed to the problem. In rural India the family division 'Bhaiya Batan' (co-sharing by brothers) badly affects the requirements of more houses. Now the traditional joint family system is rapidly giving place to single family system and social spaces go on shortening. More demand for houses affects the standard of living as well as good living conditions. In economically backward areas dwelling conditions are worsening day by day largely due to family partition. The shifting rural population towards industrial and commercial centres substantially affects both urban and the rural houses. In urban areas migration of population creates problem of shortage of houses and in rural areas they leave them in under-developed condition. Thus a large population still lives in unhealthy dwellings, many of which should properly be called slums.

## Planning

The rural housing scheme is urgently required in Bundelkhand so that living conditions may be improved. Planning should aim at the following goals : -

1. The villagers should be provided with house plans, suited to their socio-economic conditions.
2. They should be encouraged to use local building materials so that houses are not costly to build.
3. The loans should be distributed among the poor families only to improve the house conditions.
4. Vast schemes should be operated for slum clearance and for abatement of over-crowding.

After the independence the State Government has taken interest to ameliorate the rural housing conditions specially that of the depressed class of the society. A few tribals colonies for Kol, Saharia, Kabara Nat, Kuchbandiya, have been constructed in Banda, Jhansi and Chhatarpur districts. But these schemes are insufficient and lack water supply, medical, educational and recreational facilities. They are too glaring as the personal field survey shows. The entire tribal area needs more financial aid to improve the hygienic conditions. It is also essential to improve the economic and cultural levels of agricultural labourers with a small house as well as a piece of land for cultivation for each family as is being practiced in other.

The agglomeration of houses in a particular place gives a shape of settlement which has been discussed in the following chapters.

# 11

# Urban Settlements

A survey of the historical records, inscriptions and scattered ruins of fortification, reveals that Bundelkhand had enjoyed the advanced city culture from the Chandela period.

## Medieval Period

In the medieval period, strategic locations and sites were important for the town and township in Bundelkhand because the hills and the water barriers had given protection at least from one side. The high bluffs and bottle necks of the rivers were the choicest positions for Orchha, Hamirpur, Kalpi, Garh Kundar, Mau Sahaniya and other towns. Smiles A.R.E. aptly remarked in this connection that the "town usually sought a site naturally endowed with obstacles to free entry to attackers".

Before the origin of Bundela Rajputs the land and fallen into the hands of aboriginal chiefs who were not only politically vanquished but also socially and economically doomed. When Gond and Khangar chiefs came to power

Mau-Sahania and Garh-Kundar attained the status of capitals. The successive Rajput clans maintained locational advantages in feudal system. The majority of towns, therefore, were founded by Rajput chiefs and sub-chiefs in the campaigns of conquest and colonisation. Orchha and Datia towns were good example of that time which stand on the strong natural sites where Mughal armies found it difficult to approach. The chiefs erected their capital buildings in 'Rajput styles'. Kalpi, Jhansi and Hamirpur towns were other fine examples of the medieval period which still stand on high bluffs and bottle-necks of the rivers.

Bundelkhand is predominantly rural with backward industrial economy. There are 40 urban centres with a total population (2011). Except a few towns most of them are essentially small in size, having inadequate urban facilities because these are over-grown villages.

## Classification of Towns

The purpose of classification is to group urban centres of similar nature and to define the salient common feature of their growth, layout, morphology and town-country relationship. The urban centres are diversified in nature but certain functions dominate the character of each individual centre. According to census data of working and non-working groups, which is clear the former is high in Class IV and Class V towns such as Maharajpur, Bobina of Class IV and Garhi Malehra, Mau-Ranipur and Manikpur. However, the proportion of workers is low in Nowagon, Orai, Gursarai, Rath, Mahoba, Hamirpur and Charkhari urban centres where the dependency ratio is very high. The proportion of urban population is least engaged in agriculture which varies with size. It is the least in Class I and Class II and highest in class V centres. Bundelkhand towns are unbalanced in their functional differentiation, expansion and contraction of their tributary areas, because the chances of expansion of towns from the nucleus of the original site are more important for urban morphology. A particular activity in a city or town dominates the economic life of that city or town which becomes its major function. On this basic assumption the urban centres are classified as follows:

With above view, certain conclusions are drawn here with regard to the regional distribution of various types. In transitional part, agricultural towns dominate the region. Mining and household industry and manufacturing centres also dominate in the same track with a few exception which is a manufacturing centre lying in eastern plain of Bundelkhand. Public and professional services centres are district headquarters except Babina and Nowgaon. The Trade and Commercial centres Kalpi Rajapur are situated on the bank of the Yamuna river and Kaunch, between Pahuj and Manikpur are located in western and eastern parts of Bundelkhand respectively. The diversified centres are mainly located in Gneissic peneplain of the region except Orai centre which dominates the Jalaun plain.

## Urban Centres

Potantiality of urban centres shows the importance of towns and cities. It reveals that potentiality of urban centres varies on the basis of available economic indices (banks, markets, factories, etc.) and social indices (educational, recreational, cultural associations, hospitals, communicational offices, administrative headquarters and local newspaper associations) in urban centres, which attract the urban population to satisfy their requirements.

## High Potentiality Centre (5000-8000 and above)

Jhansi carries the highest potentiality in the region due to economic and social factors which control the potentiality of the city. Jhansi possesses the largest urban

(5.07 lac) population, commissionary centre of U.P. Bundelkhand, the largest communication centre and other several economic and social institutions. High potentiality area (between 100000 to 80000 lies in Datia, Banda, Mahoba, Sagar, Babina and Lalitpur centres which are connected by railroads with the cities and satisfy their needs. Chirgaon, Mau-Ranipur, Ranipur and Tikamgarh come under the high low potentiality (between 80000-50000) category. These centre are located at sufficient distance from the city but more closely attached to the cities than other adjacent urban centres. With the exception of Mau-Ranipur other centres are away from railway tracks but well connected by roads.

## Medium Potentiality Centres (10000-50000)

Three belts of medium potentiality centres in the region. Medium high (500000-10000) potentiality is found in Jalaun, Konch, Orai, Gursarai, Nowgaon, Chhatarpur and Bijawar medium size towns. These are inter-dependent on Orai and Chhatarpur district headquarters. Medium belt of potentiality (5000-10000) extends through the medium size urban centres e.g., Hamirpur, Rath, Charkhari and Mahoba and small size centres are Maharajpur, Garhi Malehra, Atarra, Damoh and Khajuraho. All of them are poor in economic and social institutions. Although Banda is Class II towns of the region, its potentiality is medium low due to the poor economic and social factors. Location of cities like Allahabad, Kanpur and Jhansi is another controlling factors, the potentiality shifts towards these big cities.

## Low Potentiality Centres (Below 10,000)

The urban centres in eastern Bundelkhand carry low potentiality due to backward economy of the land. However, Rajapur, Karwi, Baberu, Panna and Samthar Towns carry very low potentiality which have small umland due to poor resources and poor means of transportation.

## Table - 7: Classification of Urban Centres Arranged according to Size & Function Year (2020)

| Class of Towns | Population Size | Name of Town | District | Functional Type | Regional Location |
|---|---|---|---|---|---|
| I | Over 2,00,000 | **JHANSI** | **Jhansi** | **Transport** | **The western gneissic Plateau** |
| II | 1,00,000-199999 | Banda<br>Orai<br>Sagar<br>Chhatarpur | Banda<br>Jalaun<br>Sagar<br>Chhatarpur | Service<br>Diversified<br>Diversified<br>Service | The western Banda Plain<br>In midst of Pahuj-Betwa Plain<br>South-west Plateau<br>South-East upland |
| III | 50,000-99,999 | Datia<br>Panna<br>Mahoba<br>Tikamgarh<br>Chitrakut-Dham Karwi | Datia<br>Panna<br>Mahoba<br>Tikamgarh<br>Chitrakut | Manufacturing & Trading<br>Service<br>Diversified<br>Diversified<br>Turist | West gneissic Peneplain<br>Midst of Panna hills.<br>East gneissic Peneplain<br>Central gneissic Plateau<br>Chitrakut Plateau |
| IV | 20,000-49,999 | Jalaun, Konch, Kalpi,<br>Hamirpur, Rath,<br>Mau-ranipur,<br>Atarra-charkhari,<br>Lalitpur,<br>Damoh,<br>Babina,<br>Nowgaon<br>Samthar | Jalaun<br>Hamirpur<br>Hamirpur<br>Jhansi<br>Banda,<br>Mahoba<br>Lalitpur,<br>Damoh<br>Lalitpur<br>Chhatarpur<br>Jhansi | Service, Trading<br>Sevice,<br>Diversified<br>Manufacturing<br>Agriculture<br>Agriculture<br>Household Industry,<br>Diver.<br>Service<br>Service<br>Service<br>Agriculture | North-west- Plain and ravinel land<br>Yamuna-Betwa Ravine trac and Central Plain<br>Central gnessic Peneplain.<br>East-Banda Plain and East gneissic Peneplain<br>South western Plateau<br>West gneissic Plateau -<br>East gneissic Plateau<br>West gneissic Plateau -<br>East gneissic Plateau<br>West gneissic Peneplain |
| V | 10,000-19,999 | Manikpur<br>Bijawar<br>garhi-Malehra<br>Ajaigarh<br>Chirgaon,<br>Rajapur | Chitrakut<br>Chhatarpur<br>Chhatarpur<br>Panna<br>Jhansi<br>Chitrakut | Transport<br>Household Industry<br>Mining-quarrying<br>Agriculture<br>Diversified<br>Ag.<br>Househhold Industry | East Chitrakut Plateau<br>East gnessic Plateau<br>"<br>North Panna hills<br>Central Peneplain<br>Trans Pahuj-Betwa Tract |
| VI | 5000-9999 | Khajuraho<br>Ranipur<br>Kabrai<br>Jaitpur | Chhatarpur<br>Jhansi<br>Mahoba<br>Mahoba | Turist<br>Household industry<br>Mining quarring<br>Household industry | East gnessic Plateau<br>East Yamuna ravines<br>East gneissic Plateau<br>Central Plain of Dhasan |

# 12

# Rural Settlements

Settlement is man's first step towards adaption to his environment. Its stability lies in resources placed at the disposal of the community, who built it. Permanent settlements are the result of a long evolution, however the moveable dwellings are developed by the hunters, pastoralists and primitive agriculturists. No doubt, "the entire history of civilization is reflected in present forms of human settlements". The study of their evolution is advanced in terms of regional culture, with a brief survey of the previous works of the scholars who have studied the settlement problems. The study of toponymy helps to understand the nature of origin and growth of rural settlements and impact of culture on settlements. The glorious history of the region and personality cult have played significant role from medieval period. Ancient names of the places are exception. In official records the rural settlement is mentioned with the name of 'mauza' which stands for revenue purpose having definite boundaries. It is derived from the Arabic word, 'Waza' means parcels of grounds. In Hindu rural settlement is generally known as 'gaon' (village) derived from 'gram' the Sanskrit word which implies dwellings as well as parcels of land. In the same way several scholars have used some special terms for the description of the nature and distribution of rural settlements.

**Table - 8 : Distribution of Rural Settlements (2020)**

| District | Village (00-500) | Village (501-2000) | Village (2001-5000) | Village (5001 & Above) |
|---|---|---|---|---|
| Lalitpur | 268 | 108 | 10 | - |
| Jhansi | 96 | 75 | 6 | 1 |
| Jalaun | 218 | 146 | 9 | 2 |
| Hamirpur | 63 | 68 | 11 | 1 |
| Mahoba | 95 | 83 | 11 | 2 |
| Banda | 103 | 95 | 25 | 1 |
| Chitrakoot | 205 | 140 | 8 | - |
| Datia | 153 | 55 | 4 | - |
| Tikamgarh | 216 | 85 | 8 | - |
| Chhatarpur | 201 | 187 | 9 | 1 |
| Panna | 338 | 58 | 5 | - |
| Sagar | 314 | 81 | 8 | - |
| Damoh | 69 | 8 | 2 | - |
| Niwari | 136 | 24 | 3 | - |
| Gwalior | 156 | 84 | 5 | 2 |
| Satna | 168 | 82 | 4 | 2 |

Concentrated dwellings are the legacy of the past which are associated with the semi-nomadic economy. This type of settlements are situated on the various sites in the region. On the plains uniform relief has contributed to flourishing cash-crops with the addition of agglomeration of dwellings. But on the upland defence as well as the supply of drinking water are the main controlling factors of nucleation of the villages. As population increases agriculture gains importance and agricultural communities are firmly settled on the fertile soils. The size of compact village may vary from a big hamlet to a very large village having hundreds of houses. They can be easily recognised from a distance from its large groves of trees as 'neem', 'pipal', 'gular', 'mahua', 'kaith', 'jamun', 'mango', etc. The 'strong point' village are often found in less moisturized climate.

**Table – 9 : Residental Rural Settlements -2020**

| District | No of Inhabited Villages | Village at 500 -1000 Pop. | Village 1001-2000 | Village 2001-3000 | Village 3001 to above |
|---|---|---|---|---|---|
| Lalitpur | 710 | 15 | 60 | 18 | 5 |
| Jhansi | 931 | 16 | 48 | 22 | 14 |
| Jalaun | 1052 | 31 | 30 | 31 | 8 |
| Hamirpur | 612 | 22 | 41 | 28 | 9 |
| Mahoba | 515 | 24 | 25 | 46 | 5 |
| Banda | 767 | 19 | 36 | 40 | 5 |
| Chitrakoot | 677 | 28 | 36 | 30 | 6 |
| Datia | 518 | 31 | 39 | 17 | 13 |
| Tikamgarh | 905 | 33 | 41 | 19 | 7 |
| Chhatarpur | 1157 | 36 | 38 | 20 | 6 |
| Panna | 650 | 41 | 36 | 18 | 5 |
| Sagar | 865 | 44 | 31 | 19 | 6 |
| Damoh | 479 | 36 | 41 | 18 | 5 |
| Niwari | 435 | 22 | 31 | 17 | 4 |
| Gwalior | 465 | 48 | 36 | 24 | 5 |
| Satna | 422 | 52 | 32 | 19 | 4 |

In fact it is a transitional type of settlement which is found roughly between the zones of compact and of fragmented settlements. 'This type differs from the compact settlements by reasons of the existence of a few separate hamlets, usually, one or two in the 'mauza' apart from the compact'. No doubt, the intermediate type is the result of recent development because the population is neither spread in numerous detached 'purwa' or 'dare' nor is it concentrated in a single agglomeration. There may be two reasons either the increasing pressure of population in the main village or the idea of intensive use of land.

Hamlet clustered settlements are very common in both the canal irrigated areas and plateau areas of the region. In the irrigated tehsils of Naraina, Baberu, Jalaun, Konch and Moth the farmers like to settle near their fields to facilitate production while in the Tehsils of Laundi, Ajaigarh, Panna, Bijawar, Chhatarpur, Tikamgarh, Jatara and Niwari people are compelled for segregation from the main site due to the meagre means of livelihood. A separatist tendency has been marked among the low castes, who have their community hamlets near some large villages. These satellite hamlets are totally dependent on the main village for their socio-economic requirements. Sometime socially they lack cultural cohesion and unity. Hamlets are linked with 'mauza khas' (main), large village by the canal lines or by foot-paths and cart tracks for socio-economic activities.

A settlement of this type consists of a main site and several hamlets standing separate from the another. These linked hamlets are often scattered over the entire 'mauza' which are treated as a single unit for the purpose of revenue and administration. Population is dispersed into them, so that the main site becomes much smaller than the above two types of settlements. The size and number of fragmented settlements is largely dependent on the capability of the surrounded area. The number of detached hamlets per inhabited 'mauza' may vary from five to thirty.

These are the tiny foci and are located on a single geographical facility such as an embankment, a river or small piece of arable land. Generally these possess a single economic function such as agriculture, forest work, cattle rearing, mining or quarrying etc.

# 13

# Population

The study of population is necessary to understand the social morphology of a region. The distribution and density of the population is closely inter-related with the physical features which have both restrictive and permissive relations to human activities. Areas of favourable climatic conditions facilitate the people and harsh climatic conditions and rugged topography restrict the population growth, development, expansion and movement. First of all the trans-Yamuna plain gravitated the people from 'Aryavart', whenever they moved south-eastward. In those days Bundelkhand was scantily populated by the primitive people due to the dense forests undulating topography and harsh climatic conditions. The natural circumstances made them indolent, backward and slovenly in their methods and in mode of living, so the population remained stationary till the advent of the Rajputs.

Under the Chandela rulers Bundelkhand was well populated and enjoyed peace and prosperity. But after the 11th century the region became the 'cock-pit' of the powers and tranquility of the inhabitants had been disturbed from time to time. 'Villagers were normally prosperous and peasants lived a frugal life'. Population decreased either by war or migration to the adjacent regions during the bad years. Under the British rule population increased by and large because they had provided a good deal of facility for settlement by introducing canal irrigation, more transport and communication lines and ensuring the lives of the people from depredation and natural calamities.

## Distribution of Population

It is fact that Population is very unevenly distributed in Bundelkhand. Topography has a destructive contributed in its distribution patterns. A small area of the northern agricultural land is comparatively thickly populated while a large area of the southern upland is sparsely settled. The dots are clustered in the irrigated areas and near water bodies and dispersed more or les on the granitic land. Concentration and dispersion of population depend on the nature of slope, climatic conditions, quality of soil, irrigation, transport facilities, agricultural prospects and socio-economic factors. On plains the means of communication provide facility to trade and general movement of people. So concentration is quite reasonable. The population follows the streams because large alluvial fertile tracts attract the population. The black soil patches are thickly populated. Banda, Jalaun, Carry high density of population due to rich soils and irrigational facilities.

## Agricultural Density

Agricultural density is the index of general population pressure on cultivated area and carrying capacity of land. The average agricultural density of the region is as low as 187 per km$^2$. Virtually it also shows the low pressure of population on cultivated land and indicates the future prospects of carrying more population on the cultivated area. The agricultural density of the plain districts of Jalaun, Hamirpur and Banda is comparatively lower than that of eastern district of Uttar Pradesh. The total agriculture population of Bundelkhand is 81.92 percent and the cultivated land is only 52.78 percent. The districts of Tikamgarh, Banda and Panna carry the highest agricultural densities and Jhansi and Chhatarpur also carry higher agricultural densities than the regional average. The districts of Datia, Hamirpur and Jalaun have much lower agricultural densities. Generally agricultural density is higher where arithmetic density is low specially in the southern part of the region where limited arable land is available for cultivation. In Tikamgarh and Banda districts agricultural density is high due to the intensity of agriculture. As whole the arithmetic density is high in Bnada, Jhansi, Jalaun districts due to the high development of communication lines and trade and commerce.

## Physiological Density

Physiological density correlated the total population with the total cultivated land. It is quite obvious by that physiological density varies according to the total population and total cultivated area. The average physiological density of Bundelkhand is higher than its agricultural density. It is much higher in Jhansi, Banda and Tikamgarh districts as against the average density on the basis of the high total population; and lower in Hamirpur, Datia, Panna and Sagar & Damoh. Moderate physiological densities are ranged in Jalaun and Chhatarpur districts.

## Carrying Capacity

The 'economic density' according Garnier, B.B. discerns the crowding of cultivated land unit as discussed in agricultural density. However, carrying capacity discloses true balancing power of population over the total productive capacity of the land in relation to the regional total population. Here we have tried to find out the carrying capacity district-wise on the U.N.S, Stamp, L.D. basis by considering the per hectare average yields of various crops calculating the wheat-caloric-outpur equivalents. It is calculated on the basis of the standard tables of food values and caloric requirements prepared by the Indian Council of Medical Research. The average carrying capacity of Bundelkhand is calculated for persons per km.[2] The districts of Banda, Jalaun, Tikamgarh, Chhatarpur and Jhansi have higher carrying capacity than the average number. The tehsils of Naraina, Baberu, Banda, Tikamgarh, Garautha and Jalaun carry the highest capacity due to high percentage of irrigated and double-cropped land as well as good transporting facilities. The northern part of the region has enough potentialities for the future development, however, the upland region is experiencing high pressure of agriculture density. In Jhansi, Tikamgarh, Chhatarpur and Panna districts people earn their living mainly from the forests and allied activities. Datia and Hamirpur districts have the lowest carrying capacity in the region ranging from persons. Owing to relatively poor soils and lack of irrigational facilities, the progress of small scale industries based on forest and mineral resources can be able to share the population pressure with the agricultural land.

## Table - 10 : Population (2011)

| District | Total Population | Male % | Female % | Growth Rate % (2001-2011) | Sex Ratio | Density Per Km² | Average Literacy% | Urban Popul.% | Rural Popul.% |
|---|---|---|---|---|---|---|---|---|---|
| **Lalitpur** | 12,18,002 | 52.50 | 47.50 | 24.57 | 905 | 242 | 64.95 | 14.38 | 85.62 |
| **Jhansi** | 20,00,755 | 53.05 | 46.95 | 14.66 | 885 | 398 | 76.37 | 41.78 | 58.22 |
| **Jalaun** | 16,70,718 | 53.62 | 46.38 | 14.87 | 865 | 366 | 75.16 | 25.06 | 74.94 |
| **Hamirpur** | 11,04,021 | 53.76 | 46.24 | 11.09 | 860 | 275 | 70.16 | 18.96 | 78.04 |
| **Mahoba** | 8,76,055 | 53.19 | 46.81 | 15.52 | 880 | 279 | 66.94 | 11.36 | 88.64 |
| **Banda** | 17,99,541 | 53.69 | 46.31 | 19.84 | 863 | 408 | 68.11 | 15.35 | 94.65 |
| **Chitrakoot** | 9,90,626 | 53.21 | 46.79 | 23.53 | 879 | 308 | 60.52 | 09.72 | 09.28 |
| **Datia** | 7,86,375 | 53.34 | 46.66 | 18.40 | 875 | 292 | 73.50 | 23.17 | 76.83 |
| **Tikamgarh** | 10,40,113 | 52.59 | 47.41 | 20.10 | 901 | 286 | 62.57 | 17.29 | 82.71 |
| **Chhatarpur** | 17,62,857 | 53.09 | 46.91 | 19.50 | 884 | 203 | 64.90 | 22.65 | 77.35 |
| **Panna** | 10,16,028 | 52.45 | 47.55 | 18.60 | 907 | 142 | 66.08 | 12.32 | 87.68 |
| **Sagar** | 23,78,295 | 52.74 | 47.26 | 17.60 | 913 | 232 | 77.52 | 29.81 | 70.19 |
| **Damoh** | 12,63,703 | 52.27 | 47.73 | 16.60 | 896 | 173 | 70.92 | 19.82 | 80.18 |
| **Niwari** | 4,04,807 | 52.60 | 47.40 | 18.50 | 924 | 296 | 32.60 | 19.75 | 80.25 |
| **Gwalior** | 20,32,036 | 52.76 | 47.24 | 17.75 | 864 | 446 | 76.65 | 17.75 | 82.25 |
| **Satna** | 22,28,935 | 53.76 | 46.24 | 19.19 | 927 | 297 | 81.37 | 19.7š | š |

**Table - 11 : Percentage of Age Groups (2011)**

| District | Total Population | Children (0-14) | | Young (15-34) | | Middle (35-59) | | Elderly Persons (60 and above) | |
|---|---|---|---|---|---|---|---|---|---|
| | | Male | Female | Male | Female | Male | Female | Male | Female |
| Lalitpur | 12,18,002 | 21.53 | 19.04 | 17.37 | 15.41 | 11.61 | 10.33 | 2.18 | 2.54 |
| Jhansi | 20,00,755 | 21.54 | 19.02 | 17.38 | 15.40 | 11.62 | 10.32 | 2.19 | 2.53 |
| Jalaun | 16,70,718 | 21.78 | 18.94 | 17.18 | 15.79 | 11.66 | 9.89 | 2.39 | 1.76 |
| Hamirpur | 11,04,021 | 21.11 | 18.79 | 16.43 | 15.49 | 11.90 | 11.07 | 2.52 | 2.69 |
| Mahoba | 8,76,055 | 21.10 | 18.80 | 16.42 | 15.50 | 11.89 | 11.08 | 2.51 | 2.70 |
| Banda | 17,99,541 | 21.24 | 19.66 | 17.14 | 15.42 | 11.58 | 10.05 | 2.50 | 2.39 |
| Chitrakoot | 9,90,626 | 21.23 | 19.65 | 17.15 | 15.41 | 11.59 | 10.04 | 2.51 | 2.38 |
| Datia | 7,86,375 | 21.06 | 18.67 | 17.41 | 15.81 | 12.00 | 10.06 | 2.21 | 2.78 |
| Tikamgarh | 10,40,113 | 21.55 | 19.19 | 17.05 | 14.96 | 11.64 | 10.74 | 2.22 | 2.65 |
| Chhatarpur | 17,62,857 | 20.86 | 18.87 | 17.58 | 14.86 | 11.93 | 10.72 | 2.50 | 2.68 |
| Panna | 10,16,028 | 21.05 | 19.94 | 17.59 | 15.70 | 11.03 | 10.38 | 1.92 | 2.29 |
| Sagar | 23,78,295 | 21.07 | 19.95 | 17.61 | 15.72 | 11.05 | 10.36 | 1.91 | 2.28 |
| Damoh | 12,63,703 | 21.06 | 19.94 | 17.63 | 15.73 | 11.04 | 10.35 | 1.92 | 2.27 |
| Niwari | 4,04,807 | 21.30 | 19.17 | 17.25 | 13.92 | 11.50 | 10.74 | 2.20 | 2.15 |
| Gwalior | 20,32,036 | 21.75 | 19.25 | 16.15 | 14.72 | 12.30 | 11.15 | 2.15 | 1.90 |
| Satna | 22,28,935 | 21.60 | 19.85 | 16.60 | 15.75 | 13.13 | 12.50 | 2.27 | 1.95 |

## Agricultural and Non-Agricultural Workers

Agriculture is the backbone of the economy of Bundelkhand. The average percentage of agricultural and non-agricultural groups is 80% and 20% respectively. The agricultural group includes the cultivators and agricultural-labourers who are directly associated with agriculture. 'The rapid population growth and its high density, intensive use of land have resulted in a continued growth in agricultural occupation'. The high agriculture-population resides in pure rural tehsils e.g., Baberu, Mahroni, Seondha and Niwari. High agriculture-population is found in Tikamgarh, Panna, Hamirpur, Chitrakoot and Banda districts and rural workers are busy in agricultural activities. But in Jhansi district the number of rural agricultural workers exceeds in rural areas. Only Urban Centers specially in Hamirpur, Chhatarpur, and Banda districts are busy in cultivation. Besides, the above districts the percentage of urban workers who are busy in agriculture is below 20% the region. The number of non-agricultural workers is very low in the region which reflects its under-development. The high percentage of non-agricultural workers is found in Jhansi, Datia and Jalaun districts which is multifunctional due to urbanisation, advanced means of transport, communication and other public services. Now the surpluse workers can be sifted from Primary to secondary and tertiary groups for the development of the region therefore high dependency, can decreas from the primary group.

## Problems and Prospects

To estimate the population problem by the number of the people alone is not enough at present time, for their quality must also be taken into account. This qualitative concept regarding the possibilities of food resources, the demand of commodities and standard of living focuses on the major problems. Because the whole economic system even in its qualitative elements goes hand in hand with the degree of civilization and popular psychology. The people of Bundelkhand realise that their standard of living is too low and cherish the hope of improving it. That is why there are local and regional migrations. The distribution of population on the land. Nearly the regional areas are sparsely populated and shows that there is no high pressure of population in the region. Where 'positive checks' have shortened the growth of population as well as the food resources from time to time. The low sex ratio is another important factor of population which have restrained the growth and have created a social problem in the region. The real problem, which the region experiences, is the heavy agricultural dependence, low productivity of land and high death rate. For raising the living standards it is essential to increase the production per unit of land. Certainly there are still extensive areas which canbe brought under the plough and production can be increased by advanced farming techniques, crop rotations, irrigation and trasport facilities. The standard of living can also be raised by industrialisation, educational and medical facilities because they will increase the working capacity of the population and reduce the heavy mortality rates. So it is necessary to develop both the branches of economy: agriculture and industry, simultaneously. Industrial development will attract the country folk from filling the soil due to high wages. In this way pressure of population will be shifted from primary sector to secondary and tertiary sectors. On the other hand the surplus man power also will be fully utilised. Advanced technology promises more food production, but the fulfilment depends on the adjustments of the regional: social, economic and political organization.

# 14

# Agriculture

The Bundelkhand region is basically agricultural and rural. A majority of population (in 2011) depends on agriculture. The proportion of agricultural dependence increases in absolutely rural tahsils e.g., Baberu, Mahroni, Seondha, Laundi, etc.. The unfavourable physical conditions with socio-political insecurity have deeply affected the life of common people as well as the regional agriculture. In spite of the official efforts and improvements agriculture remains backward to all intents and purpose.

The percentage of cultivated area has steadily increased since independence. The percentage variation of net sown area during five years 2020 is 60.86 percent, because more fallow land and culturable waste land has been undertaken. However, a large area of southern upland is forested and waste land. On account of low percentage of cultivated area in this part, the pressure of population is high on land especially in Tikamgarh and Panna districts as compared to the low land districs.

## Major Crops

A number of crops are grown in mixed form, but a few of them are important to be noted here for acreage as well as production. Food crops have a direct bearing on the productive land and the distribution of population; whereas the commercial crops lag far behind because these (sugar-cane, cotton, tobacco, oil)

### Table - 12

### Land Utilization (%) Year (2020)

| District | Total Geog. Area (in Hect.) | Not available For cultivation % | Forest % | Cultivated waste land % | Non-Agriculture use % | Barren Land % | Total Cropped Area % | Area Sown More Than Once % |
|---|---|---|---|---|---|---|---|---|
| Lalitpur | 5,07,500 | 8.15 | 5.10 | 23.75 | 1.75 | 6.45 | 54.80 | 15.00 |
| Jhansi | 51,329 | 6.90 | 1.05 | 10.15 | 8.40 | 5.50 | 68.00 | 16.90 |
| Jalaun | 4,54,434 | 8.00 | 0.05 | 0.25 | 0.55 | 1.15 | 90.00 | 15.60 |
| Hamirpur | 3,90,178 | 5.20 | 4.15 | 3.18 | 3.15 | 5.22 | 79.10 | 16.50 |
| Mahoba | 3,27,429 | 6.15 | 6.50 | 3.50 | 10.05 | 1.00 | 72.80 | 14.50 |
| Banda | 3,38,767 | 4.20 | 2.68 | 2.50 | 4.15 | 6.37 | 80.10 | 12.05 |
| Chitrakoot | 3,95,874 | 6.40 | 5.65 | 13.25 | 14.75 | 8.65 | 51.30 | 16.40 |
| Datia | 2,95,874 | 16.80 | 9.28 | 2.80 | 2.25 | 0.87 | 68.00 | 17.00 |
| Tikamgarh | 3,47,740 | 12.50 | 6.50 | 11.75 | 12.75 | 8.70 | 47.80 | 13.70 |
| Chhatarpur | 8,63,036 | 13.75 | 8.75 | 12.25 | 11.50 | 6.95 | 46.80 | 24.80 |
| Panna | 7,02,924 | 18.25 | 25.25 | 4.15 | 2.00 | 15.15 | 35.20 | 12.60 |
| Sagar | 10,22,759 | 20.10 | 23.75 | 0.60 | 1.15 | 1.70 | 52.70 | 19.10 |
| Damoh | 7,28,583 | 25.15 | 22.50 | 1.10 | 2.40 | 5.15 | 42.70 | 26.8 |
| Niwari | 1,56,262 | 5.70 | 6.15 | 10.15 | 12.75 | 7.15 | 46.25 | 14.15 |
| Gwalior | 8,03,014 | 11.15 | 12.15 | 7.43 | 11.15 | 7.95 | 46.15 | 13.15 |
| Satna | 7,22,830 | 11.35 | 20.15 | 13.15 | 12.15 | 7.15 | 45.45 | 12.16 |

## Wheat

Wheat is an important Rabi crop of Bundelkhand, sown during October/November and harvested during April/May. It is grown in well drained loamy-clayey and black soils. Cool and warm-dry climate is suited to it. Rainfall ranges between 50 and 100 cms. but irrigation is necessary for good yield in the north-west tract where meager rainfall is received during the cropping season. Now after 1980 it is sown widely in the area and gives a bumps production. Kathia & Pisia variaties are sown in black soils (without irrigation) and clay and loamy soils (with irrigation). These are grown, more than fifty percent in un-irrigated land with gram and barley. A number of improved varieties are introduced in both U.P and M.P. Bundelkhand. The Agricultural Research Institute also introduced Pusa varieties. Sonoro-64 largely grown in low fertile soils with tanks and well as sources of irrigation in Tikamgarh and Chhatarpur districts. During 2020 the production is the highest in Orai, Moth, Konch and Maudaha tahsils. Total production in also high in the low land areas including Jhansi, Hamirpur, Jalaun and Banda districts and lowest in Panna, Chhatarpur, Datia, Sagar & Damoh districts. Since the introduction of canal irrigation Bundelkhand has become an important producer of wheat. With the exception of irrigated areas mixed cropping-pattern is mostly prevalent in dry farming areas. As its acreage is increasing by and by, production is also going up. In the wheat growing areas the rural land-scape is well developed and more prosperous. Here population is fairly distributed over the areas and village are medium to large in size.

### Jowar – Bajra

Jowar-Bajra are the inferior grains as well as chief millets of the region, which are mostly used as food by the poor and partly as fodder crops. These are Kharif crops, widely sown in the region in the months of July-August and harvested in November. Irrigation is not needed this crop. Usually mixed cropping pattern is practiced with moong, arhar, urad, till (sesamum) and andi (castor).

### Barley

It is the next staple food crop which is sown in dry climate and light soils. As compared to wheat, it needs a more porous soils and also can tolerate alkalinity. It shares about 6 percent area of cereals. Generally barley is grown with wheat (gojai) and gram (bejhar). Rape, mustard and linseeds are produced with it. Cultivation practices and climatic conditions are the same to some extent as for wheat.

## Rice

Rice production is gaining popularity in the region because it is grown more or less in every part of region. It occupies 10.2 percent area of food crops; highest in Naraini, Banda and Tikamgarh, Panna, Sagar & Damoh tahsils and lowest in Panna and Ajaigarh districts. The hot and humid climate and the fertile alluvial and black soils of the lowland provide an ideal environment for its cultivation. Rice plant has very wide physiological adaptability, so it is grown in both the southern and the northern parts. Autumn rice is grown in unirrigated tahsils, far and wide, while the winter rice is chiefly produced in the Ken and the Betwa canals irrigated areas of Banda and Jalaun districts and Tubewells, tanks and wells irrigated areas of Tikamgarh and Chhatarpur, Jhansi, Sagar districts. Rice cultivated areas are thickly populated because its cultivation requires a lot of manual labour and settlements are dispersed from semi-compact to hamletted pattern. In some places these areas face water logging problem which can be got rid of by providing extra canals.

## Oil Seeds

Bundelkhand is basically a food producing region. The oil-seeds, other commercial crops e.g., sugarcane, cotton, tobacco, spices etc. are insignificant. Truck-farming meets only the local demands. But Baruwa Sagar is the biggest centre of vegetable production from which the vegetables are transported to different regions. Mahoba and Malehra are famous for the betel cultivation. Since the introduction of tube-wells vegetable and fruit production has largely increased in the countryside. Sugarcane and tobacco are cultivated in irrigated areas but these crops have no commercial values due to limited production. Their acreage is increasing year by year, while cotton, opium, indigo 'al' etc. are losing their grounds due to absence of industries. The physiographic and climatic conditions, irrigational facilities and the farmers' interest and requirements of the folk are the main controlling factors of distribution of commercial crops in this part of the country

**Table - 13 : Area under main crops (in %) 2020**

| District | Cereals millets | | Pulses | | Oil Seeds | | Food crops | |
|---|---|---|---|---|---|---|---|---|
| | 2001 | 2011 | 2001 | 2011 | 2001 | 2011 | 2001 | 2011 |
| Lalitpur | 48.7 | 30 | 43.2 | 62.0 | 5.6 | 6.7 | NA | 0.2 |
| Jhansi | 61.7 | 34.4 | 24.0 | 56.8 | 10.0 | 3.9 | NA | Neg |
| Jalaun | 40.1 | 38.3 | 51.1 | 54.9 | 6.2 | 4.0 | NA | 1.0 |
| Hamirpur | 48.0 | 33.7 | 43.4 | 60.9 | 6.7 | 3.0 | NA | 0.9 |
| Mahoba | H | 26.7 | H | 64.8 | H | 7.0 | NA | 0.1 |
| Banda | 61.0 | 56.0 | 36.0 | 41.1 | 11.6 | 1.4 | NA | 0.8 |
| Chitrakoot | B | 56.5 | B | 39.7 | B | 2.1 | NA | 0.6 |
| Datia | 45.6 | 36.7 | 41.2 | 43.5 | 10.0 | 16.0 | 0.8 | 1.0 |
| Tikamgarh | 62.0 | 36.1 | 15.7 | 25.3 | 8.7 | 23.0 | 12.0 | 5.2 |
| Chhatarpur | 54.0 | 36.2 | 24.3 | 39.1 | 9.8 | 9.8 | 10.7 | 2.9 |
| Panna | 66.3 | 48.3 | 18.0 | 46.0 | 14.4 | 4.4 | 0.1 | NA |
| Sagar | 56.7 | 25.7 | 21.8 | 43.5 | 12.1 | 25.3 | 11.3 | 3.8 |
| Damoh | 57.5 | 24.7 | 29.5 | 39.9 | 8.9 | 10.2 | 11.3 | 3.8 |
| Niwari | - | 31.25 | - | 14.14 | - | 21.15 | - | 2.35 |
| Gwalior | 54.15 | 23.15 | 21.36 | 46.15 | 14.76 | 21.95 | 10.25 | 1.46 |
| ©° ° | ^ | TM | ^ › | TM Š | ^^ TM | › Š | ^^ TM | TMŠ |

## Irrigated Area

The total irrigated area by all means during 2011-20 vary from 24 to 64% The variation between the figure is the result of the scarcity of water. Canals provide 50% irrigation and wells & tubewells and tanks other means of irrigation are follow.

## Table - 14 : Percentage of Irrigated Area (2020)

| District | Total Cultivated Area | Total irrigated Area | Total % of irrigated Area 2011 | Total % irrigated Area 2019 | % of irrigated food Area crops. | % of irrigated Non food crops. |
|---|---|---|---|---|---|---|
| Lalitpur | 3,85,426 | 2,10,013 | 54.5 | 49 | 49 | 51 |
| Jhansi | 4,65,240 | 2,23,027 | 47.9 | 25 | 25 | 75 |
| Jalaun | 4,37,205 | 1,91,399 | 43.8 | 42 | 42 | 58 |
| Hamirpur | 3,52,531 | 1,11,508 | 31.6 | 64 | 64 | 36 |
| Mahoba | 2,92,021 | 1,14,949 | 39.4 | 47 | 47 | 53 |
| Banda | 4,22,544 | 1,74,065 | 41.2 | 50 | 50 | 50 |
| Chitrakoot | 1,93,321 | 53,450 | 27.6 | 29 | 29 | 71 |
| Datia | 2,20,465 | 1,36,302 | 59.6 | 40 | 40 | 60 |
| Tikamgarh | 1,98,922 | 1,00,426 | 55.8 | 78 | 78 | 22 |
| Chhatarpur | 51,319 | 2,26,581 | 44.3 | 65 | 65 | 35 |
| Panna | 2,97,655 | 84,420 | 28.4 | 24 | 24 | 72 |
| Sagar | 7,10,690 | 2,36,635 | 33.3 | 28 | 28 | 72 |
| Damoh | 3,98,648 | 1,14,138 | 28.6 | 40 | 40 | 60 |
| Niwari | 1,71,720 | 1,06,352 | 55.3 | 30 | 45 | 36 |
| Gwalior | 3,89,865 | 1,84,720 | 55.6 | 41 | 33 | 34 |
| Satna | 3,70,186 | 1,36,138 | 54.2 | 39 | 36 | 35 |

## Major Irrigation Projects

The streams, rising from the Vindhyas, are not snowfed, hence discharge of water in winter becomes short when the rabi crops need it. Gravity canals coming out of the reservoirs like Goving Sagar, Saprar, Kabrai, Rangwan, Arjun, Matatila, Kamla Sagar, Kachreh, Magarwara and Pachwara and irrigate a considerable area of the region. After independence both the state Governments (U.P and M.P) have taken several major and minor irrigation projects. The important projects are as follows:

### Lalitpur Dam (Govind Sagar)

It has been contructed on Shahzad river in Jhansi district to irrigate an area of 54000 hectares in Jhansi, Jalaun and Hamirpur districts, to raise the productin of about 18,000 metric tons of addition food grains. Its storage capacity is 4420 million cubic feet. The length of canals is 45 Kms. by which water drains to the fields. The object of this dam was to supplement the supplies of water to the Betwa canal.

### Saprar Dam

This is constructed on the Saprar river a tributary of the Betwa in Jhansi district which is about 8 Kms. south of Mau-Ranipur town. Its storage capacity is 3800 million cft. of water. That is sufficient to irrigate an area of 26000 hectares in Hamirpur and Jhansi districts to produce about 20,000 metric tons of additional food grains. The stored water is being utilised for irrigation on the Dhasan canal system since 1951.

### Kabrai Dam

This project is working in Mahoba district near Mahoba town. It stores 500 million cft. of water for irrigation of 3000 hectares of land around Mahoba and Mahoba tahsils. Kabrai dam has its own significance in this area because in the spring season the water table becomes low and means of irrigation are also very poor.

### Rangwan Dam

The Rangwan Dam was necessitated to increase the supply in the Ken canal system. It irrigates an area of 50 thousand hectares in Banda district. The site is an Banne river a tributary of the Ken about 8 Kms. away from the existing Gangau dam in the Ken canal division. By now all the channels under the project have been constructed and opened for irrigation.

### Arjun Dam

The dam is constructed on the Arjun river, a tributary of the Betwa about 2.4 Kms. south-west of Charkhari town in Mahoba district. The storage capacity is 2550 milion cft. from a catchment area of 200 Kms. It provides irrigation facilities to 15800 hectares of area in the district.

Jamini, Ohan, Chandrawal, Kyolari and other minor irrigation schemes are working near by.

## Mata Tila Project

It is multi-purpose project for irrigation and power. It is constructed between the two rocky ridges close to the Betwa Valley flowing over gneissic basement in Jhansi district. The dam impounds 50,000 milion cft. of water and irrigate an additional area of 205000 hectares of U.P. and M.P. The catchment area of the dam is 15800 Kms. and the length of new canals is 1316 Kms. It is one of the biggest power projects of U.P. The capacity to generate power is 40 million Kws.

### Table - 15 : Live stock Percentase under Main Categories(year 2020)

| District | Total No. Cattle | Cattles | Buffaloes | Sheep Goat | Poultry | Pigs |
|---|---|---|---|---|---|---|
| Lalitpur | 8,05,402 | 52.72 | 20.33 | 18.36 | 8.08 | 0.37 |
| Jhansi | 2,52,206 | 30.89 | 19.15 | 27.83 | 19.61 | 1.47 |
| Jalaun | 8,04,254 | 27.79 | 26.6 | 35.74 | 6.20 | 3.30 |
| Hamirpur | 6,53,277 | 39.67 | 20.42 | 23.67 | 12.27 | 3.84 |
| Mahoba | 5,76,451 | 33.31 | 17.86 | 30.93 | 13.38 | 4.47 |
| Banda | 8,38,080 | 42.02 | 27.76 | 19.67 | 5.33 | 2.13 |
| Chitrakoot | 7,09,102 | 59.93 | 19.58 | 16.17 | 2.79 | 1.45 |
| Datia | 4,19,556 | 30.08 | 33.96 | 30.44 | 4.63 | 0.85 |
| Tikamgarh | 6,78,852 | 40.28 | 16.82 | 30.16 | 11.84 | 0.68 |
| Chhatarpur | 11,41,667 | 43.78 | 13.78 | 31.52 | 9.14 | 1.68 |
| Panna | 10,75,057 | 49.53 | 18.26 | 17.88 | 11.92 | 2.16 |
| Sagar | 9,30,909 | 6357 | 14.49 | 11.67 | 9.28 | 0.64 |
| Damoh | 7,96,298 | 64.58 | 12.71 | 13.48 | 8.09 | 1.03 |
| Niwari | 4,03,136 | 52.2 | 33.46 | 14.45 | 3.36 | 0.14 |
| Gwalior | 11,05,106 | 53.3 | 22.45 | 13.36 | 4.45 | 1.36 |
| Satna | 9,11,197 | 52.36 | 24.35 | 27.45 | 3.16 | 1.95 |

## Suggestions For The Improvement

Some suggestions can be given for the development of the regional live-stock industry. These are as follows :

1) The animal husbandry farm should be opened in every district of Bundelkhand.

2) The number of veterinary hospitals must be increased considering the number of live-stock and these centres should be connected with fair weather roads.

3) The key-village breeding scheme of the government should be operated in Madhya Pradesh Bundelkhand too.

4) 'Go-Shala' (a new Shelter for Cattle) scheme of government carried one in every district and Tahsil with sufficient aid.

5) Large dairy and small co-operative industries should be opened in the region.

6) The traditional methods and techniques of milking and ghee making should be replaced by new advanced scientific techniques.

7) Publicity and training centres of live-stock industry are necessary for enlightenment of the people.

8) Grass and fooder must be stored for crucial periods by the government because the region has bitter experience of natural calamities.

9) Improved type of bulls should be fairly distributed in the region.

10) The slaughter of young, useful and productive bovines must be checked. Now the scientific and mechanisation agriculture descourage the live stock husbandry as well as cottage industries.

# 15

# Transport

Bundelkhand occupies the central position in the country and it lies across the main arteries of Indian commerce running east-west as well as north-south. However, it faces the transport problem for its economic and industrial development due to its rugged topography. Smiles, A.E. "physical configuration effectively establishing route patterns and indirectly influencing the economy, has naturally a great bearing on the nature and character of transportation". There are some large pockets and several unabridged rivers and streams where roads and railways are lacking for accessibility. Therefore, such areas are facing difficulty in importing the manufactured goods or exporting the raw materials. In fact, Bundelkhand is one of the under-developed regions where transport and communication facilities are inadequate for its economic development.

## The National Highways

The national highway Sagar-Jhansi-Kanpur is running parallel to Kanpur-Jhansi railway-line. It is approachable from Jhansi by a pontoon bridge at Kalpi at a distance of 22

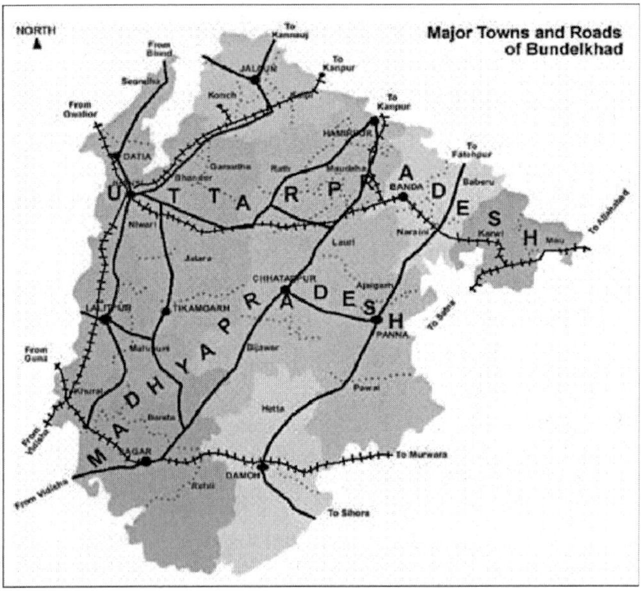


Kms. It connects Lucknow and Jhansi via Kanpur and the length is 301 Kms. and Jhansi-Sagar by 198 Kms. The chief towns on highways are Lalitpur, Jhansi, Orai and Kalpi. A branch is bifurcated from Jhansi to Shivpuri which is 99 Kms. long. The second National Highway passes from the eastern part of the region, from Allahabad to Jabalpur. From Panna to Rewa it is the 140 Kms. long. It links Bombay, Hyderabad and Nagpur chief cities of south-west India and Varanasi, Patna and Calcutta in the north-east.

## The State Highways

Before the Britishers there were few all weather roads. They broke the isolation by vehicular traffic opening with the several metalled and unmetalled routes which functioned as major intra regional links. The road lenght of southern Bundelkhand is not available because M.P. Bundelkhand was diffused into several petty states upto the formation of Vindhya Pradesh. The total lenght of metalled and unmetalled roads in U.P. Budelkhand was 1246 Kms. and 3997 Kms. respectively. But in post-independence period the road length of the region has highly increased, both the metalled and unmetalled roads (3049 Kms. and 4430 Kms. respectively. Now according to 2020 data the total length of roads and rail not is 12556 and 4815 kms. respectively. The roads are the main arteries of communication in Panna, Chhatarpur and Tikamgarh districts where rail lines are absent to move the traffic of people, general merchandise, clothes and forest produces.

## The Local Roads

A number of metalled and unmetalled roads are either under the public works or Zila Parishad or Municipal Board or Forest and Canal Departments. These have local importance. Roadside avenues are maintained along many roads. These roads have been divided into six categories. The first and second classes roads are metalled. The others are only fair weather roads. The length of forest roads vary in accordance with the area of forest divisions, the nature of surface and the nature and volume of the traffic which they carry.

## Accessibility

Accessibility emphasizes the importance of place because it provides an instrument to measure the effectiveness of a transportation cover. Bundelkhand was one of the inaccessible parts of India mainly because of its physical build and remained undeveloped for a long time. But the introduction of rail-roads has enhanced its accessibility to in great extent.

It is quite apparent that road accessibility is very high in Bundelkhand in comparison to the rail accessibility. The roads (national and state high ways) are widely spread throughout the region. These criss-cross the land north-south and east-west. In spite of a large distribution of roads over the land, there are still numerous big and small pockets where inaccessibility is experienced. The size of pockets increases from north west to south-east. The southern part of Bundelkhand is well served by roads; even then the areas between Chhatarpur and Tikamgarh, Mahroni and Bijawar, Tikamgarh, Damoh, Sagar and Lalitpur, Chhatarpur and Bijawar, Chhatarpur and Ajaigarh and Mahoba and Nareni live far away from main highways. Except in the north-western part there are several small and large inaccessible pockets scattered over the low land. These lie between Karwi and Baberu and the Yamuna banks, Banda and Hamirpur, Mahoba and Maudaha, Rath and Hamirpur, Rath and Mau Ranipur, Rath and the Betwa banks and Jalaun and Jagammanpur. Accessibility is greater is Jhansi, Banda, Orai, Mahoba, Mau Ranipur, Lalitpur and Chhatarpur and other central places of the region. Most of the areas along the river courses are only seasonally accessible because of the unabridged streams. As a whole the southern Bundelkhand is inaccessible areas have been pushed to the periphery of the plateau which is covering a large part of south-west part of the region

## Rail Transport

In 1880 the necessity of extensive and rapid transportation was urged by the 'famine Commission'. During 1885-87 the Jhansi-Manikpur railway branch was opened. A trunk line 'The Great Indian Peninsula Railway' connects Itarsi-Agra via Jhansi. Another branches meet in the same system from Kanpur to Jhansi and Manikpur to Jhansi.

The region was in dire necessity of minimization of the hazards of famine. Moreover, the quick military movements and the need of sound administration were the other factors for the rail reticule growth. The Central Government established the 'Central Railway Zone' at Jhansi where three lines lead in a fork pattern from Bombay to Delhi via Jhansi,

Jhansi to Kanpur and Jhansi where three lines lead in a fork pattern from Bombay to Delhi via Jhansi, Jhansi to Kanpur and Jhansi to Allahabad. The lowest density of stations is found especially in ravine belt. The distance between two main stations often varies from 96 to 120 Kms. But in the plain area several new stations have been opened.

## Rail Network

The average rail road per lakh population is sufficiently low (20.18 Kms.) which covers 23.0 Kms. per thousand Kms. The district-wise rail lenght per thousand sq.Kms. and per lakh population is comparatively high in Jhansi (24.0 Kms.) and Banda (19.50 Kms.) districts and low in Datia, Jalaun and Hamirpur districts. Except Datia district M.P. Bundelkhand is completely devoid of railways.

## Water Transport

All the Vindhyan streams flow through the rocky beds and deep narrow valleys. None of them are navigable from the economic point of view. In the pre-rail the Yamuna was considered the main artery for trade and commerce in the Northern India. It carried a lion's share of trade and commerce from one region to another. So it was the life stream for the 'areas existing to the west and the east of the Yamuna, has been a region of perennial cultural evolution throughout the historic lines'. In the past therefore, the river was utilized as means of transportation of heavy and cheap goods. Now it is still used as water-way to transport fodder, sand stone an fire wood from one place to another. The advent of rail and road development has reduced the importance of water transport. Canals are used only for the irrigational purpose and their roads are used by bullock carts and pedestrians.

## Air Ways

Before the Khajuraho aerodrome Panna was the landing strip of I.A.C flight from Delhi to Khajuraho. During the tourist season a weekly service was made available upto Panna for carrying tourists to Khajuraho. Now on every day air service is available, from Delhi to Khajuraho. Available statistics show the fluctuating number of tourists - Indians and foreigners. Remarkably from 1961 when the Khajuraho airstrip was completed the number has been increasing year by year. With the exception of Khajuraho aerodrome no such air service is available for the region. But navigational aids and emergency night landing facilities are available at Lalitpur town for night air-mail service between Delhi and Nagpur. Another aerodrome is proposed to be located near the north-east of the Chitrakoot Dham-Karwi.

## Table - 16

## Railway Lines & Road Net (Year- 2020)

| District | Population 2011 | Area Kms. | Total Rail Meterage Km | Roads in Kms | Rail Road (in Kms) Per lac population | Rail Length per 000sqr. |
|---|---|---|---|---|---|---|
| Lalitpur | 12,18,002 | 5039 | 236 | 756 | 22.30 | 21.25 |
| Jhansi | 20,00,755 | 5024 | 640 | 1857 | 24.20 | 24.00 |
| Jalaun | 16,70,718 | 4566 | 297 | 1065 | 13.70 | 18.00 |
| Hamirpur | 11,04,021 | 4021 | 456 | 1109 | 24.10 | 3.40 |
| Mahoba | 8,76,055 | 3144 | 356 | 987 | 27.30 | 4.16 |
| Banda | 17,99,541 | 4408 | 455 | 1159 | 19.50 | 23.20 |
| Chitrakoot | 9,90,626 | 3216 | 316 | 965 | 18.40 | 22.15 |
| Datia | 7,86,375 | 2995 | 118 | 156 | 14.00 | 14.00 |
| Tikamgarh | 2,60,315 | 3885 | 91 | 576 | 19.40 | 18.50 |
| Chhatarpur | 17,62,857 | 8687 | 604 | 870 | 27.40 | 28.50 |
| Panna | 10,16,028 | 7135 | 224 | 634 | 20.10 | 18.15 |
| Sagar | 23,78,295 | 10252 | 536 | 1365 | 15.36 | 16.56 |
| Damoh | 12,63,703 | 7306 | 356 | 1057 | 16.58 | 17.25 |
| Niwari | 4,04,807 | 1170 | 130 | 220 | 4.75 | 3.45 |
| Gwalior | 20,32,036 | 4560 | 224 | 770 | 17.35 | 16.95 |
| Satna | 2228935 | 7502 | 603 | 640 | 21.35 | 19.76 |

# 16

# Trade

Bundelkhand trade is primarily based on the produce of agriculture, forest, mineral and livestock wealth. But a great difficulty is faced in getting the export and import data of these commodities. Jhansi is the biggest centre of emporium and traffic as which gives a vivid picture of inwards and outwards good of 2020. Moreover, the region is well known for Ayurvedic medicines, brass works and paper industry. Export of Bundelkhand are mainly based on the fields and forests.

The agricultural commodities dominate the markets. Mostly the surplus cereals, pulses and oilseeds are exported to the neighbouring states. Oilseeds are transported to Kanpur, Bombay, Hapur, Prayagraj and Delhi. First of all these commodities are collected from 'mandis' (grain markets) through the 'arhtiyas' (wholesale commission agents) then export to the main marketing centres of the country. Mau-Ranipur, Chirgaon, Lalitpur, Jhansi, Jakhaura, Madhogarh, Jalaun, Orai, Kalpi, Banda, Atarra, Baberu, Badausa, Rath, Maudaha, Bharua-Sumerpur, Mahoba, Harpalpur, Prathvipur, Tikamgarh, Jatara, Chhatarpur, Bijawar,

Mahrajpur, Laundi, Datia, Seondha, Badoni, Panna Damoh and Sagar urbans are the largest trading centres since the British occupation.

Mahoba is still a chief trading centre of 'Pan' (betel leaves) which is largely exported to the countryside as well as important centres of northern India. Barua Sagar is another main exporter of vegetables.

The rural economy is no more self-sufficient. The increasing products of agriculture, forest and mineral resources, transport and communication facilities and industrial outputs have accelerated the regional trade and commerce. But that is confined within the land due to inadequate means of transport absence of enterprise, industrial backwardness, poor raw materials and low standard of living.

The prosperous 'a' dying industry, cotton goods, and rural crafts have declined because the railways had begun to carry the bulk of the manufactured goods and markets were flooded with imported goods like salt, sugar, rice, cloth, medicines and so on from the countryside. The local trade of agricultural products, forest and mineral wealth and animal raw materials were only concentrated in the region which merely fulfilled the local demands.

Gradually, the pace of trade increased but during thirties and forties trade declined on account of general economic depression. After the second World War the pace of economic recovery was accelerated and several new industries came into existence. The process continued and with the achievement of independence, more and more people took interest in trade and commerce.

The southern region is rich enough is forests and forest products. Annually a handsome revenue is collected from the forest products of Tikamgarh (6 lakhs), Chhatarpur (10 Lakhs) and Panna (12 Lakhs). Manikpur, Bijawar, Panna,

Lalitpur and Ajaigarh are the important timber exporting centres. Tendu leaves are exported to Prayagraj, Satna, Amroha, Niwari, Mumbai and Indore for 'biri' making centres.

Panna diamond is well known. It is mined from Majhgawan and Ramkhiriya. The chemicals for Paint and Varnish industry are imported from Bombay, Kanpur and products are exported to Calcutta, Agra and other important centres. Building stone is largely exported to Kanpur, Agra, Allahabad, Lucknow and Faizabad centres. The region is rich is livestock but due to the lack of bone and leather manufacturing industries the bones, hides and skins are exported to Kanpur, Agra and Bombay. For instance, Datia district exports 15 to 20 thousands hides and skins annually and Chhatarpur 119 thousands and Panna 50 to 60 thousands follow the trend. Woolen raw materials are sent to Kanpur, Agra, Mirzapur centres since there is no woollen industry.

Ayurvedic medicines are transported to the countryside from Jhansi, Lalitpur, Mau-Ranipur, Kulpahar centres. Jhansi produces medicines worth about Fifty lakhs annually which is largely exported. The raw materials are obtained from Kanpur. Agra, Delhi, Calcutta, Lucknow and Bombay. For brass works of Jakhaura, Chhatarpur and Srinagar the raw materials are imported from Mirzapur, Kanpur, Calcutta and Bombay places. From Kalpi paper and cardboard are sold to the government offices at Prayagraj, Gwalior and Kanpur centres. Handloom clothes are mostly consumed locally and some one exported to Chanderi, Ahmedabad, Gwalior, Kanpur and Bhadohi for printing works. With the above view the region is rich in the natural resources and has best possibilities for the industrial development.

## Trading Centres

Bundelkhand is a land of fairs and festivals. The local

fairs, market (haats) and bazaars play an important role in regional trade and commerce. These are the main business centres for the inhabitants which cater to the daily needs of the people. some of them have large lands were the businessmen collect from large distances and have their daily, seasonal and annual requirements. Some of these centres are good marts of cattle, food grains, vegetable, ghee, clothes, daily use articles, countrymade shoes, etc. But mostly the trade is of retail type. In some of the urban centres, district and tahsil headquarters daily markets meet but in a few urban and rural centres weekly and bi-weekly market are held. In the local fairs and market the retail traders of all sorts pay their trade.

The regional trade is mostly confined within Uttar Pradesh and Madhya Pradesh. Kanpur is the largest supplier as well as consumer of the above commodities. Agra, Bombay, Prayagraj, Calcutta, Delhi, Ahmedabad, Gwalior, Lucknow, Jabalpur and Mirzapur are other notable places from where import and export flow. All the consumers' goods like cotton piece goods, sugar, salt, medicines, cigarettes, matchboxes, kerosine oil, leather goods, cement, iron, machinery, electrical goods etc. Are greater in demand with increasing population as well as cultural contacts. Trade can flourish more with the development of transport and communication lines and growth of industrialisation and urbanisation in the region.

# 17

# Industry

The history of Jhansi city, under the Bundela chiefs relates that there was a large industry for smelting the iron ore. In 1874 there were fifty three furnaces at work. Brassware work also very old in the region which was carried on at Chhatarpur, Mau Ranipur and Srinagar (Mahoba). Bundelkhand is industrially backward, although it has surplus agricultural produces and rich in raw materials. Lack of enterprise and technical knowledge and paucity of skilled labour are the main constraints on industrial growth in any region. Now the outlook of the people has started changing. Their inhibition against starting industries is steadily declining due to motivational campaigns undertaken in the area, inducements and incentives offered by both the state governments, to start small scale industries, liberal credit facilities made available on preferential terms by the specialised financial agencies. Technical know-how and the skills are also being made available by spread of education, greater mobility of factors of productivity within the region and increasing contact with the areas.

## Large Industry

The Baidyanath Ayurvedic Bhavan (Ltd.) and the India

Hume Pipe Co. are the large scale industries in Bundelkhand in which the invested capital is Rs. 29 lakhs and there are 415 persons employed. The former was established in 1948 at Jhansi which produces medicines worth about Rs. 20 lakh annually. The power supply is obtained from the Matatila dam. Chemicals and other industrial requirements are imported from Kanpur, Agra, Delhi, Calcutta, Lucknow and Bombay. The prepared goods are transported through the rails and roads. The central location of Jhansi city and producing drugs and herbs are the potential factors for its location.

## Medium Industry

There is only one unit of spirit industry on medium scale in the region, located at Chhatarpur. The annual production capacity is 33,51,535 litres.

## Flour Mills

'Atta' (flour) mills are widely distributed over the region. Before availability of electricity all such units were run by steam engines. In fact some located in remote parts are steam-powered. In case of house-hold industry, one or two rooms accommodate the establishment in the residential house and the unit is run with the help of the family members. Their market does not extend beyond the locality where industrial unit exists.

## Dal-Mills

Pulses are largely grown in Bundelkhand, which cover 16.2 percent of cropped area. Gram is widely transported from the region to other important marketing centres of the country. In U.P. Bundelkhand there are five dal mills functioning combined with flour, rice and oil mills. Four of them are located at Atarra and Banda, one at Jhansi and two at Kalpi. Later two units of Kalpi are independent and established with the investment of rupees 6 lakhs. Six workers are employed. Other three units are established in

Tikamgarh district which are running with the rice mills with investment of rupees one lakh each. The total number of daily workers is more than 50. In Datia district 8 units of dal and oil mills are working with 80 workers.

## Oil-Pressing Industry

There are seven oil mills at work in Jalaun district in which a capital of more than ten lac is invested and 18 workers are employed. In Jhansi 5 Units are functioning with an investment of 20 lakhs and 133 workers. In M.P. Bundelkhand a number of small oil units are running. The number of oil units is as follows: Tikamgarh 15 with 416 workers, chhatarpur 24 with 513 workers, Panna 25 with flour mills and Datia 8 with dal mills. Due to the lack of large pressing units a large quantity of surplus oil seeds is sent out of the region.

## Textile Industries

### *(i) Cotton Textile*

The handloom industry is an important industry of Bundelkhand in which about 4 lakh families are dependent for their livelihood. There are 19046 weavers engaged in 16153 looms under 15 societies in the Jhansi division. Dyeing and printing works are also carried on in 51 units mainly at Jhansi, Mau-Ranipur and Lalitpur centres with 1300 workers. The raw materials are imported from Agra, Bombay and Kanpur. This industry is run by the indigenous weavers such as 'Koris' and 'Julahas'. They produce mainly coarse cloths which meet the local needs of the villagers. In M.P. Bundelkhand 25 handloom units are working in which more than six hundred persons are engaged.

### *(ii) Silk Industry*

A 'Swadeshi Silk and Ribbon' industry was established in 1952 at Jhansi with an investment of rupees 1.76 lakh.

About fifty workers are busy in production of hosiery goods and ribbon worth 2 lakh rupees annually. The fashion of Kosa-silk bearing are changing year to year and demand decreases due To power fabrics.

### *(iii) Wollen Industry*

Kalpi was the biggest centre of woollen industry in the region. In most of the household women and young children are busy in spinning and weaving sweaters, mufflers, blankets, etc. The 'Julahas' are very good at it and about 60 families are entirely dependent on cottage industry. The contractors supply the raw materials and export the readymade goods to Kanpur and other local markets. About 78 spinners are at work in Hamirpur district. The coarse blankets and woolen carpets are woven at Jhansi, Talbehat and Lalitpur by the indigenous experts. There are six registered woolen mills working in Jalaun district, on investment of Lac. One unit of blanket making industry has been established at Jhansi. Woollen spinning and weaving work is also carried on in Datia and Tikamgarh.

### *(iv) Leather Industry*

Bundelkhands is very rich in raw materials for leather industry because surplus hides, skins and tanning materials such as 'babul' dark and fruit of 'ghont' tree which are largely transported to Bombay, Kanpur and Agra. Leather works are mostly managed by 'Chamars' (Kuril) in both, the rural and urban areas. Now it is facing competition with the modern leather industries.

## Brass Work

Chhatarpur has been the biggest centre of metal works in Bundelkhand for a century. At present hundred families of artisans with a total of 1200 workers are busy in metal works. The ward of 'Theaters' in Chhatarpur town in still known as 'Tamari ward'. The raw materials are imported from Mirzapur, Kanpur, Calcutta, Bombay and abroad. At Chhatarpur 'Burma Metal Industry' is functioning since 1956. It is run by power and the number of daily workers is 20 to 100. Manufacturing and nickling works are carried out on improved methods. Srinagar (Mahoba) is the second biggest centre of brass works where 8 registered brass utensil units are functioning with an investment of ten lakh rupees. Srinagar still has main-tained its reputation in manufacturing brass dolls and utensils. Three units are working in Jhansi district with an investment of one lakh rupees, employing 33 daily worker. Jakhaura (Jhansi) is an important centre of brass work where several households are busy in this work. In the Fourth Year Plan two brass work schemes have been proposed at Chirgaon and Birdha in Jhansi district. Panna, Tikamgarh and Banda are the other important centres where brass wares are manufactured.

## Iron and Steel Industry

Large iron-smelting industry was run by 'Lohar' (blacksmith) in Jhansi district. Bijawar series have rich soft-haematite iron ore pockets. Blacksmith is done by village artisans who manufacture crude and ordinary agricultural implements and common hardwares on payment of a certain amount of crops given at harvest time. These families engaged in blacksmithy partly depend on agriculture.

## Wood Works

Apart from the saw and furniture mills three wooden toy units are functioning at Sitapur-Chitrakoot (Banda). In one of them Rs. 60 thousands has been invested and others are simply cottage industries. In Panna district 25 wood-comb making units are at work in which 50 workers are engaged. Soft variety of wood such as dudhi, semal and salai is patently supplied from the neighbouring forests. The demand for plywood and prefabricated house materials is increasing in day to day life.

### Biri Making

Tendu leaves are available in plenty and are exported to Jabalpur, Allahabad, Satna, Amroha, Bombay and Indore. The total number of biri making units in Bundelkhand is 40 which are functioning at important centres viz., Jhansi, Chirgaon, Ranipur, Lalitpur, Mahroni, Tikamgarh, Chhatarpur and Manikpur where about two thousands workers are engaged.

### Kattha Making (Catechu)

The Khair (acacia catechu) tree is plentily available in the Bundelkhand forests. In the interior of the dense forests Khairwar or Khairwar families are seasonally employed in Kattha making on contract basis. Kattha is extracted from the heart of the Khair Wood by soaking, boiling or steaming its pieces by a primitive method. A few societies and several units are working in Chhatarpur and Panna districts.

### Reed, Bamboo and Cane Work

Basket making is an extensive industry of Bundelkhand. Reed and bamboo baskets are largely made by the people of low castes. They are very skilful in bamboo works : making hand fans, baskets, mats, 'chik' (curtain) etc. Bamboo work is fashioned by them on the traditional lines. It is doubtless that bamboos satisfy a variety of human needs. Tenements are built of bamboo and furnished with bamboo stools, chairs, tables and beds which are supplied locally and to the urban markets. Besides these articles, bamboo and reeds are largely used as thatching materials. Three bamboo societies are at work in Panna with 30 workers, seven in Tikamgarh with 120 workers and ten in Jhansi district. In a large area of Ranipur (Chitrakoot), Devendra Nagar (Panna), Bijawar (Chhatarpur) and Deogarh, Talbehat, Madura (Lalitpur) bamboo clumps have been planted by the forest departments.

## Paint and Varnish

It is one of the flourishing industries of Bundelkhand because the region is rich in raw materials. There are seven units busy in production of colours in which Rs. 35872 of capital is invested. Jhansi is the biggest centre of it there 5 units are at works. The chemicals are imported from Bombay, Kanpur, Calcutta and Agra and the products are largely transported to important markets of the country.

## Paper and Card Board Industry

Paper industry is century old at Kalpi which is the biggest centre of paper production in Bundelkhand. Thirteen units are functioning : 8 private and 5 under 'Khadi Board'. The number of daily employed workers in each unit is 8 to 25. Annual production is 25000 rims, worth about 4 lakhs. They produce varieties of paper such as blotting paper, drawing paper, filter paper, writing paper, file cover and others. Raw materials are imported mainly from Kanpur and Bombay. Other facilities such as market, skill labour, transport, technical guidance etc. are locally available.

## Ayurvedic Medicines

There are five ayurvedic medicine units functioning in Bundelkhand, based on local raw materials. These units are located at Jhansi, Lalitpur, Orai, Kulpahar (Hamirpur) and Datia. About 100 persons are directly employed.

## Scented Tobacco

Two units are manufacturing scented tobacco at Mauranipur and Banda towns. The annual producing capacity is worth Rs. 80,000 and Rs. 60,000 respectively. Another unit of 'Tansen Pastilles' (which is chewed with betel for their flavour) is located at Jhansi which manufactures goods worth about Rs. 75000 annually.

## Pan

'Pan' industry of Mahoba has long standing prestige. Its location by the railway track facilitates trade. Previously it was largely exported to Lahore, Peshawar, Naini Tal, Kumaun, Rajputana, Banaras and several other market centres of Northern India and the return amounted to Rs. 16 lakhs per annum. The betel cultivation is entirely in the hands of 'Baris' and 'Tamolis' for centuries. Baldeogarh (Tikamgarh), Mahrajpur and Malehra (Chhatarpur) and Pali (Jhansi) are the other famous places where extensive cultivation of betel leaves is practiced. Several families of Baris and Tamolis are directly dependent on this industry for their livelihood. It 'Pan' is utilised to extract the 'Pan essence' it will be more paying to the Tamolis than the 'Pan' trade itself.

## Industrial Prospects

Considering the material resources, the region has great prospects for industrial development. However, the majority of population is dependent upon agriculture. Its chief trade consists of exporting the raw products of agriculture, forest and minerals and import of the manufactured goods from outside the region. On the basis of available raw materials local requirements and transport facilities some new industrial units can be established. Newly developed road-net work and availability of electricity have largely extended the future prospects of industrialisation. Bundelkhand has ample scope for cottage and medium scale industries. The village and cottage industries should be brought on the modern lines and old fashioned tools must be replaced with improved equipment which will increase the efficiency of the workers as well as production. The possibilities for industrial development may be considered in the following broad group : resource - based industries i.e. (1) those based on indigenous raw materials (agricultural, livestock, forest products and minerals); (2) non-resource based industry, which include industries based largely on materials brought from outside the region and also all manufacturing after the primary processing or extraction of natural raw materials.

## Non-Resource Based Industries

The non-resource based industries are basically local in character which have no bright prospects due to the lack of market and technical know-how. These difficulties can be over come by organising technical training centres in the region. The skilled workers will establish the metal based industries such as utensils, domestic appliances, bicycles and bicycle parts, industrial goods like wire nails, belts and nuts, screws, agricultural implements, hardware, hand tools, tin containers, small machine tools, water pipes sanitary fitting, tyre retreading etc.

# 18

# Tribes

The region was an abode of the migratory jungle tribes like Savaras and Nishadas from the prehistoric period. Before the advent of Aryans the land was originally occupied by the 'out caste' and 'low caste' people like the Kol, the Gond, the Bhil, the Bhar, the Cheru, the Kachhi, the Chamar, etc. Then the tract was densely forested and sparsely populated. But Chandela Rajputs and others vanquished them by force of arms, for instance, in the 'Shardul Charit' it has been mentioned that the Bagri and Mauha Thakurs destroyed about 7500 clans of the Kol, the Bhar, the Bhil, the Gond and others near the Kahra villages in the west of Banda district in 1137 (1080 A.D.). Such incidents confirm the presence of Tribals and indicate that they have been numerically reduced from time to time by the Rajputs who compelled them to yield and reduced themselves to servile livelihood conditions and ousted some fo them to the Vindhya hills and forests, where they lived for centuries and developed their own way of life due to inaccessibility of the areas and remained unaffected by the main stream of civilization.

At present the tribals of Bundelkhand chiefly reside in the forests and hilly areas of Lalitpur plateau and the Panna and the Vindhyachal ranges. The dominant tribal group of Mundarian and Indo-Dravidian origin are represented by the Sonrs and the Sours (40.3 percent), the Kols (21.5 percent), the Gonds (16.5 percent) and others (13.8 percent). According to the census 2011 the total populations is about one lakh, which shares 1.53 percent of the regional population.

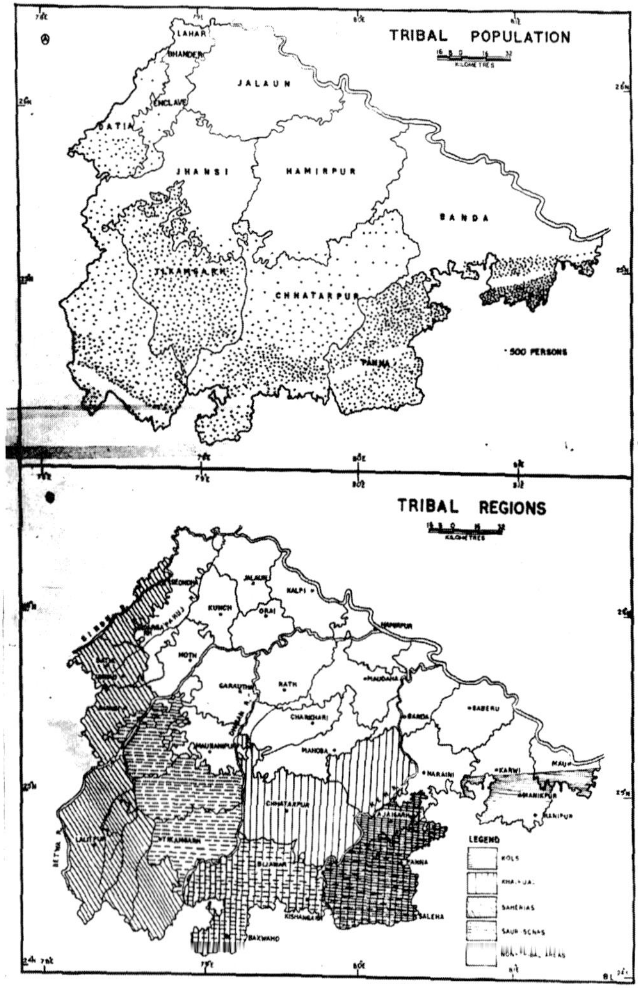

This is the most depressed section of the Hindu society, which belongs to non-Aryan stock by its physiognomy characteristics. In appearance these tribes are distinguishable by their flat features and dark complexion. But their new generations indicate somatic changes due to the cultural contacts and admixture of Aryan blood. As a whole they are very near the Protoustraloid in physical characteristics. They speak their own dialects of 'munda family' e.g., Koli, Gondi, Bhili, etc. They maintain their own socio-cultural institutions. Besides, accessibility, education, cultural relationships and economic uplift programmes of the government have brought a new change in their socio-economic life.

They are primarily busy in subsidiary activities like mining and quarrying, wood cutting, tendu leaves plucking, hunting and food collecting, which are the main sources of their livelihood. According to 2011 census majority of them is engaged in agriculture and agricultural labour (72.6 percent) and a low percentage is engaged in mining and quarrying (7.5 percent), household industry and manufacturing industry (2.8 percent), construction (.9 percent), Trade and commerce (.6 percent), Transport (.1 percent) and other services (15.5 percent).

## Table - 17

## Tribal Population in % 2011

| District | Tribes Percentage % | S.T. population % | Child Sex Ratio ST | Litracy Rate % | Literacy St. % |
|---|---|---|---|---|---|
| Lalitpur | Neg. | 5.88 | 955 | 54 | 23 |
| Jhansi | 0.06 | 0.19 | 967 | 67 | 45 |
| Jalaun | Neg. | 0.05 | 1129 | 65 | 48 |
| Hamirpur | Neg. | 0.04 | 660 | 61 | 24 |
| Mahoba | Neg. | 0.07 | 870 | 57 | 19 |
| Banda | Neg. | 0.01 | 789 | 57 | 33 |
| Chitrakoot | Neg. | 0.04 | 667 | 55 | 47 |
| Datia | 1.60 | 2.00 | 912 | 63 | 43 |
| Tikam garh | 2.25 | 1.85 | 587 | 64 | 33 |
| Chhatarpur | 3.50 | 4.00 | 946 | 55 | 34 |
| Panna | 15.4 | 13.0 | 926 | 63 | 37 |
| Sagar | 9.70 | 10.0 | 943 | 63 | 45 |
| Damoh | 12.6 | 13.0 | 973 | 60 | 44 |
| Niwari | 2.05 | 1.15 | 320 | 54 | 21 |
| Gwalior | 3.15 | 1.75 | 768 | 64 | 42 |
| Satna | 4.35 | 3.16 | 897 | 53 | 34 |

After independence, during the Five Year Plans the government, both the Central and State have been taken special interest in the welfare and development of tribals and for their assimilation with the countrymen by education, financial assistance in agriculture and cottage industry and rehabilitation projects.

Of course, the State Governments have introduced many structural and institutinal changes by abolishing the intermediaries. But so far as Bundelkhand is concerned it remains virtually unaffected by those progressive measures. Where bonded labour systems such as 'Harwaha', is very much prevalent, that amounts to slavery of tribals in the hands of non-tribals.[1] The regional big landholders, money-lenders, contractors and well-to-do persons still exploit them by all means. With the contacts of the civilised society and the aid of government welfare schemes a light of development is being seen among them.

## The Kols : A Sample Study

The Kols along with other Mundari Tribes, are original occupants of Bundelkhand, who were driven by Rajputs to the Vindhyan land. They predominantly reside in the south-east part of the region, especially in the Vindhyachal and the Panna ranges, consisting of Mau, Karwi, Ajaigarh and Panna tehsils.

## Origin

The various customs, religious practices and physiognomic characteristics reveal that the Kols are one of the Kolarian group of races because the Kolarians at one time occupied the vast area of the Northern and Central India. Indeed there are good reasons to believe that the Savaras were formerly the dominant branch of the great Kolarian tribes in the north and east and the Gond in South. To the east of the Savara belt were the Kol, Baiga and other allied tribes in the Kaimur - Vindhyan hill, with a great extension towards Chhota Nagpur and possibly even beyond". With the above view the Kols are an offshoot of the Mundas of Chhota Nagpur.

As far genesis of the word 'Kol' is concerned, the several etymological sources are being mentioned by the researchers. Campbell Sir G. 1887 remarked that the generic name 'Kolas' or 'Coles' usually applied to the aborigines of the hilly country of Chhota Nagpur, Mirzapur and Rewa where they predominantly live. It is also said that 'Kol' is derived from the Mundari words 'Ho', 'Hore' means 'man'. In course of time these words corrupted in different forms as 'koro', 'kolo' and 'kol'. In Sanskrit literature 'Kola' means 'a hog' which was applied by the Aryans to the original inhabitants of the country which means a 'pig killer'. Etymologically Kol or Kola consists of 'Ki' and 'la' meaning 'mountain home' of the tribal districts.

Not with standing the etymological differences Kol is a Mundari Tribe and lives mainly in the central zone of the country. Most of the Mundarian races claim a common ancestor but they differ in socio-cultural institutions. It is doubtful if the Kols of Bundelkhand are the descendants of 'Sevari' of Ram Charit Manas, whos was a Bhil woman. Above all Kol is one of the food gathering and hunting jungle tribes of the region. Their habitations are called by the non-tribals as 'Kolaan' and their woman folks are pointed out as 'Kolins'.

## Racial Features

On a critical appraisal of different opinions of scholars it can be concluded that the Kol is a Mundarian tribe. Dr. A.C. Haddon writes about the racial features of Kalaria group. They have a dark-brown, almost black skin, coarse black hair incline to curly and scanty beard, low medium stature. They are dolichocephalic, cephalic index (74.5-76) with a low narrow forehead, irregular features, thick lips, eyes often bright and full and not oblique, and the nose broad and flat (Nasal Index Korwa 92.5) Munda 89.9, Kharwar 89.7, Santhal 88.8, Bhumij 86.5) - these all are platyrrhine".

In appearance they are of medium stature and dark in colour but Crooke W. 1891 has remarked about Mirzapur Kols that they are a very dark race, their features are hardly so coarse as those of the Majhis or Kharwars. Many of the Bundelkhand Kols have broad and flat noses and oval faces. The hair is straight and black but some have curly or wavy hairs. The eyes are small but bright. Forehead is small in breath and length. The chin is usually not well developed and lips are thick. The growth of hair forming beard and moustaches is scanty. The average height of males is 1.62 meters and that of females is 1.50 meters. As a whole their features are coarse; rarely a handsome face is to be seen. The unhealthy physiognomic conditions, early marriage, hard work and malnutrition lead to poor health of the women folk. The men are also lean and thin in their structure. With the coming of new faces the complexion is quite fair with prominent chins, delicate lips and big bright eyes and other non-tribal physical characteristics are obvious to the admixture of Aryan blood.

## Demographic Features

The Kols are concentrated in the 'Central Tribal Belt' of the country mainly in Chitrakoot, Prayagraj, Mirzapur and Varanasi districts of Uttar Pradesh. The Kol shares 22 percent of the total tribal population of U.P. and 5.1 percent in M.P. According to the census of 2011 the Kol population is 18,934 which consequently increased to nearly 25,000 in seventies. Chitrakoot and Panna districts are the largest agglomerations of the Kols in the Bundelkhand region, whereas their colonies are scattered on the plateau areas of the Vindhyachal and the Panna ranges in the east of chitrakoot and Panna districts.

Practically, it is difficult to trace out a continuous growth of their population because in Uttar Pradesh they were listed among scheduled castes since the first census. They have been notified as scheduled tribe by a Presidential order in 2011 only.

They numbered 3698 in Banda Chitrakoot districts. In

twenties their population increased to nearly six thousand, but within seventy years they have multiplied more than four times. According to a block-wise survey conducted by the Harijan and Social-Welfare Department of U.P. (2011) the Kols population is 15219.

The working percentage of Kols is much higher (61.6) than the non-tribal working population because both the male and female belong to working class. They are per excellence agricultural labourers. The cultivator (14.8 percent), agriculture labourers (46.4), mining and quarrying (6.9) account for about 72.1 percent of the total workers. The table below works out of details. Household industry includes Manufacturing, Construction, Trade and Commerce, Transportation activity are nil by Kols.

Literacy is absolutely nil among the Kols population due to socio-economic reasons. But the number of students is increasing in the seventies with the execution of reclamation programmes.

## Physical Landscape

Kols are predominant in the Patha tract of Chitrakoot district, consisting of Manikpur, Mau and Mau Tehsils. Some of them also in the hilly land of Ajaigarh and Panna tehsils. The whole plateau and hilly area is surrounded by the river Yamuna in the north, separates Allahabad district in the east, the Vindhyachal and the Panna ranges in the south-east and south west which negotiates with the hilly tracts of Rewa and Satna districts. In the west the Paisuni and the Ken delimit the boundary lines. It covers an area of about 2500 sq. Kms. With the average height 300 meter above the sea level.

Physiographically the tract is a sub-division of the Vindhyan upland, composed of sand stones, limestones, Shales, Bundelkhand granites, quartz reefs, metadol evite etc. Besides the gems of Panna, These rocks are devoid of metalliferous deposits but important for human use where they live. As we have stated in the preceding pages that the Vindhyan lands have yielded the first building stones which are famous for their beauty as well as durability. On this land these aborigines are busy in quarring, stone cutting and forest works. The topography of the tract is of undulating character which retains the features of dissected plateau. There are two escarpment of the Vindhyachal range and the Panna range. The slope of the table land lies on both the sides - north-east and south-west. The drainage pattern follows the slope of escarpment. A numerous seasonal rivulets criss-cross the land and utimately meets the Yamuna in the north-east and the Ken in the south-west. The river Bardaha, Rundh and Medash are the main tributaries which facilitate the lives in this part. But is summer season water scarcity becomes acute, due to the high runoff, non permeable rocks and high water table therefore So droughts and scarcities often occur.

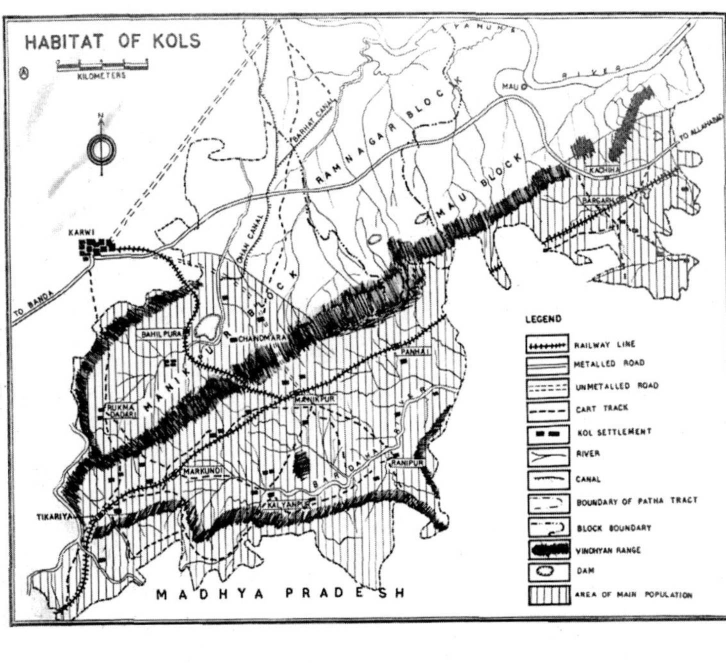

Both the ranges are covered with the scrubs and fine deciduous forests. Patha area accounts for 19.9 percent under forest and 21.4 percent is waste land and Ajaigarh and Panna range amounts to 30 percent under forest and 20 percent is waste land. A series of beautiful gleans, luxuriant vegetation one comes across along with rich hunting grounds. These deciduous forests are under the forest department, where these people are employed in wood cutting, tendu leaves plucking and other forest works. They depend on the forests for their livelihood and building materials.

The sub-tropical type of climate is largely governed by its physical features. The harsh-dry and humid climate is the result of its topography and vegetal cover. The mean annual precipitation varies between 80 and 100 cms. and temperature from $12^0$C in winter to $30^0$C in summer. Sometime it reaches $48^0$C causing havoc to lives and property.

The soil which is composed of scrambled sandstones, is of poor quality carrying low capacity and bearing less capability of cash crop production. In most of the areas the thickness of soil is very less due to the rocky strate. Small millets - jowar, bajra, kodo, sanwa, ragi, etc. are abundantly produced.

As regards transportation, a large part of the area is inaccessible. Lucky in Patha area two railway branches meet at Manikpur : one is Prayagraj - Itarsi - Bombay branch of the Central Railways, Bargarh, Manikpur and Markundi are the important railway stations. Another branch from Allahabad to Jhansi, bifurcating at Manikpur junction. Bahilpurwa station is an important tribal concentration being left side of this track. But the area of Ajaigarh and Panna is far away from railway lines. Only a few metalled and many fair weather forest roads are main arteries. Several metalled and Link roads have arise cross the Patha track in the present century.

## Economic Pursuits

Their economy is deplorable. They live hand to mouth because they are being exploited by the big farmers, money-lenders, contractors and other rich people of the areas. They are landless mostly, labourers. They may be grouped into three categories : (1) cultivators, (2) agriculture labourer and (3) non-agriculture labourers.

They work in the fields for the big farmers and landlords and get some share (usually one sixteenth of a little more than that in 'Harwaha' system agriculture) of the harvest. In share cropping system, those who have a pair of bullocks, get one and a half of the production included seeds, etc. They practice primitive type of agriculture. Rainfed crops are mostly grown in this part of land due to in fertile soils and lack of irrigation. In Patha tract 32.7 percent is total cropped area, out of 3.1 percent area is sown more than once. But in south-west this percentage is slightly increased as 40 percent area is sown and out of which 7 percent land is double cropped. The agriculturist population in Patha area is 819 and in south west 310.

They are not good agriculturists because they are lethargic and have no taste in agriculture. When they have enough food to eat, they do not like to do any type of work. Majority of them is engaged in agricultural activities as labourers. Men, women and children, all participate in sowing, harvesting and other agricultural works.

Forest and quarries offer good opportunities of employment. When they are free from the agricultural activities in the month of April, May and June, they pluck the tendu leaves and collect the minor forest products for their livelihood and sell them in the neighbouring market centres. In the rainy season they are employed by the contractors to cut the jungles on low wages. Their economy, no doubt, is controlled by the non-tribals. These contractors and landlords exploit them, do not pay adequate wages to them. Sometimes they also get employment in quarrying centres.

All hard and assiduous duties like protecting the crops in cold nights, ploughing, erecting the hoses, hunting, cutting the woods etc. are done by men and light works are performed by the women. Often Kolins do light outdoor labour of non-tribals. Defacto, ladies are supposed to be more responsible than men. Generally they become victims of 'begar' or forced labour by non-tribals. Hasan (A.) 1972 has aptly remarked about their condition that "the Kols live life of helplessness, not knowing how to get out of the web woven around their lives by the vested interest".

They never like to take up any menial professions such as shoemaking, pig-rearing, etc. While they are treated as untouchables by the orthodox Hindu society. Hunting and fishing are other supplementary sources of subsistence but not a profession.

## Settlements and Houses

### Settlements

The Kol villages have a characteristic hamleted pattern called 'Purwa'. They are tiny foci, carrying modest agglomerations of 15 to 30 households. But a large number of villages have mixed population of tribals and non-tribals. The hamlets of a village are scattered from one another at a distance of one to three kilometres and are linked with cart-tracks or paths trodden by man and his beast of burden. Forest or cultivated or culturable waste land intervence between them.

In the region settlements can be grouped into three forms. The first, the pure tribal settlements are situated in the thick forest. Such tribal habitations are very few in number. The second, farm settlements, are located near the farms of big farmers who brought them to settle there to work as form hands. In such hamlets an agent of landlord, called Karinda lives and supervises the Kols. They are treated as hired workers or slaves who live in huts on the outskirts of the hamlets or they form a hamlet of their own and farmer's 'Chhaoni' is built at a little distance away from their habitation. Gidurha and Amchur Nerua can be cited as examples of such settlements.

The third mixed settlements, lie on the plain areas. In such settlements, the proportion of non-tribal population is high. However, the Kols usually live in separate hamlets, but not treated as servant of a particular family. Mixed settlements are common in Mau, Chitrakoot, Manikpur, Ajaigarh and adjacent areas.

Before the promulgation of forest by-laws their settlements were essentially ephemeral features of the landscape, because o the migratory habits of the people. reveals that the highest deserted villages lie in the south-east skirts of the region where tribal population is predominant.

The locational factors which they mainly consider are the proximity of the jungles and the availability of drinking water. Water is an important factor which guides the settlement patterns. Field survey reveals that the huts are huddled near the water bodies. Now the arable land is also taken into consideration for choosing the settlement sites. They avoid the low lying and water logging areas. A number of large settlements exist of favourable sites to be deserted by people on account of superstitions, epidemics and other adverse factors.

The settlements are compact in shape. The huts are arranged in such a manner that a common courtyard is formed between three or four huts. The open courtyard is used for common purposes such as community meetings, drying forest produces, marriages, stocking, sleeping in te summer nights and recreational purposes. The forest settlements are fenced by the thorny bushes and shrubs and wooden ballis, to save them from the depredation of wild animals.

## Houses

Generally they live in the rudimentary hutments which gives an idea about the availability of house material nearby and of the inhabitants' migratory nature. They erect their houses usually with the help of wild grass, 'Khar' and dry leaves, bamboo as well as hay. The wall materials are generally reeds or bamboo and grass, however, sometimes plastered with mud. The height of walls does not exceed 3.5 to 4 metres. The roof is made of two pieces of thatch frames joined together in a conical shape, so that is the middle of the hut one can hardly stand. The size of room varies from 6 to 10 meters long and 3 to 4 meters wide, that is used by the whole family for all purposes such as living, sleeping, cooking and storing the things. The door is marked in the middle of the front wall which is a meter wide and one and a half metre high. In place of wooden door they use the hedge called 'tatiya' or 'tatar'. A single family of husband, wife and children usually resides in a hut. Those have large families and are well-to-do, add one more similar hut and tie the cattle is a separate hut. These huts are unsafe, temporary and unhygienic, without any ventilation.

They erect their hutments in winter and summer months. The building materials are collected after the rainy season from the forests. Before the rains in May and June, they repair their huts. Majority of them lives in the huts but a few families have Kaccha houses with tilled roofs. The walls are made of mud and stone and roofs are framed and tiled. Kols never think about the house-planning, but usually they erect it in rectangular shape. No regularity is followed about their orientation. On special occasions they wash their with white or yellow orchers.

It will not be out of place to describe the Kol's colony

planning, which is constructed under the village Housing Scheme. Each house has two main rooms and a verandah in the front and a backyard. The walls are built of bricks or stone and plastered with mud and the roof is tiled. But planning differs in some colonies such as Bargarh and Kalchiha colonies in Mau Bloc. The usual pattern is a verandah in front, a room or two in the middle and a inner verandah at the back, facing towards the courtyard. In Sarhat and Bargarh colonies an additional room of cattle has been provided at the back of the house. The cost of such houses ranges between Rs. 1500 to Rs. 2000.

**Food**

It is difficult to describe their staple food. They manage to get hardly two meals consisting of dal, roti and rice. Coarse grains like gram, jowar, bajra, barley are very common, which meet their need of taking heavy diet. Wheat is considered luxury which is consumed on special occasions. Most popular pulses are arhar, gram and masoor. A form of rice is made from sawan, kodo, kakun, 'dhuniya' and wild paddy known as 'pasahi rice'.

Mahua flowers have important place in the meal of Kols which are found in abundance in the region. A large quantity of dry flowers is collected and preserved for slack seasons. The rains is the worst season of the year, because they often face starvation due to the absence of savings and long spells of joblessness. Mahua flowers are uses in multi form in their breakfast and meals.

They usually eat twice a day in the morning and in the evening. When they are at work, they take 'kalewa' or breakfast before lunch. The evening meal is called 'biyari' or 'byalu'.

Kols are fond of meat eating but they do not take all kinds of flesh. In communal ceremonies marriages and some festivals meat, liquor and tobacco are freely used.

## Dress and Ornaments

Their common garment consist of a 'dhoti', 'kurta' or 'bandi' (half shirt) and a small piece of cloth, known as 'gamchha' or 'Safi' (scarf) for headgear. During winter some of them put on 'jawahar' Jacket, 'Mirjai' made of cotton but majority wears double old shirts because they cannot afford to buy woollen cloths. Both men and women wrap their bodies is 'Chadar'. In summer season men use only a banyan or bandi to cover the upper portion of the body. They use the contry make shoes because they walk through the jungles.

The female costume consists of saree or dhoti and jhoola or blouse. Many of them do not use any undergarment beneath the sarees, and bodice. On special occasions they like to wear 'lahanga' and 'chunri' which are popular among them.

## Ornaments

Every Indian woman, tribal or non-tribal loves ornaments. They are too poor to have golden ornaments. Rarely a woman gets to wear all types of silver ornaments. Ornaments made of 'gilt' and other cheap metals are very common which carry less cost. Glass bangles and silver necklace called 'Sutia' are very popular. The ornaments in every day use are 'Sutia' (neck), Harraya (hands), Kara and Chhare (feet), Churva (hands) and Bahuta (upper arms). Other ornament such as Kardhani (waist), Jorehira (feet), Bulak (nose) Karnphool and Airang (ears) are used on special occasions.

## Other House Materials

A few families have comfortable residential quarters. They possess aluminum cooking utensils, one or two cots, mats and one or more grain bins prepared from mud. They have no proper beddings. Bed consists of chaddar, durete, coarse blanket or razai and Gaddi.

They do not possess many agricultural implements. hal (wooden plough), Kudal or Phauda (spade) a Khurpi (a small digging appliance) and Hansia (sickle) are very common which are found in their homes.

Cattle wealth represents the economic status of the Kol family. They mainly rear the calves. Cows and goats are also kept by them for milk. Very few Kols have their own bullock carts, which are mostly obtained from non-tribals.

## Social Organisation

Socially every tribal organization is broad based. In fact Kols have no pyramidal structure of society based on superiority of castes as is in vogue in Hindu society. The subdivisions of Kol enjoy equal social status. But is rural landscape land cattle wealth play an important role in determining the status of a family in the society.

## Sub-Divisions

According to Hindu caste system they have no concept of gotra etc. They are divided into numerous endogamous Kuris. Bundelkhand Kols are divided into two main socio-religious groups, the Thakurias (Thakur, a 'lord) and Ravatiyas or Sevaris (Rewat, a 'prince). There is also a minor sub-division called Mawayyos or Mawasi found in Mangawan, Markundi and Bahilpurwa neighbouring areas. Socially Mawayyas are more related to Ravatias than Thakurias. Further south-east, another sub-division is found, called Mahtiyar (Mahto, a 'leader'), which are known as Dahiat (villagers). The inter-marry with the above sects on equal terms. According to their claims and counter-claims it is uphill task to decide their superiority on the basis of sub-divisions as is the belief of almost every tribe. The names of other sub-divisions are as follows: Budbar, Baiga, Gudbar, Dehati, Dhaba and Munda.

## Panchayat

'Panchayat' is the powerful tribunal which maintains order and discipline. Every group of tribals has communal Panchayat governed by tribal customary laws. It decides all problems regarding marriage and morality and triflying disputes of the community. Panchayat is headed by the 'mukhia'. The 'mukhia' is elected by a general consensus in a democratic way. He is not hereditary but is one who is an intelligent older, commands universal respect, and financially well off. There is no limitation of time of his posting. He may hold the post as long as he is able to enjoy the confidence of the community. Misconduct and dereliction of duty may not be permissible. Whenever a dispute arises 'mukhia' nominates a panel to decide it. The size of panel depends upon the seriousness of the case. There is no fixed time of meeting. The meetings are convened when the brethren assemble at marriage or funeral feasts or when serious offences are committed by somebody. Usually it is held in the month of Baisakh (May-June) or Jeth (June-July) when people are comparatively free. The place of meeting is selected near a 'Devasthan' where water is conveniently available.

The Grand Panchayat takes cognizance of grave offences and serious disputes concerning sex, abduction, kidnapping etc. It controls and supervises the social, religious and cultural affairs of the tribe. The decisions of Panchayat are compulsorily obeyed, otherwise it leads to serious consequences. Those who violate or disobey, are treated as out-caste. They are boycotted from the rest of society from inter-drinking and inter dining. However, they do not repay the imposed penalty decided by the Panchayat.

The usual punishments imposed by Panchayat is 'bhoj' or 'roti' or fine in cash, which is given to the other party or is spent in feeding the 'biradari'. In serious offences 'bhoj' and fine both may be imposed.

## Marriage

Among the Kol marriage is universal. Only bachelors are those who are miserably poor and are unable to pay the brides' price. Only unmarried Kolin is one, who suffers physical defects. Infant marriages do not practised due to poverty. When the couple attain puberty the marriage is solemnised. Child and negotiated marriages prevail among the Kols which is the direct impact of non-tribals. But the selection of life partners is entirely dependent on the young people concerned. The average age of marriage of girls is between 8 and 12 years and boys between 10 and 16 years. Remarriage are also frequent among the Kols.

A custom is prevalent among the Kols that the father of groom searches for the bridge which is unusual in the Hindu society. Polygamy is prevalent in the Kol families and is not a social taboo. In special cases Kolin selects the second partner herself who is called 'ghar baitha' after the demise of the first husband. She can also seek redress through Panchayat if she is aggrieved by the first husband. Divorce is permissible in the Kol society. Both the parties are free to take separation from each other and to remarry if Panchayat sanctions divorce, otherwise one who keeps the second Kolin will have to pay back the marriage expenses to the previous husband which is imposed by the Panchayat.

The marriage ceremonies are performed according to the Hindu custom with minor modifications. Marriage party usually goes on foot. In the marriage of Thakurias Nai (barber) and Brahman (priest) also participate. Although endogamous, marriage is not posible between members of two different sub-divisions, some of Ravatias or Thakurias accept a girl of the other subdivision but do not agree to wed their daughters to the other sub-divisions. In some cases a part of bridge-price is paid in advance when bride's parents are extremely poor. The bride's 'bidai' among Ravatias and Thakur las takes place after the 'Gauna' or second marriage ceremony when the girl has attained puberty. Sometime the marriage and 'gauna' ceremonies are combined when the bridge is above twelve years. The 'gauna' usually is performed in the month of Aghan (December and January) an in the 3rd, 5th or 7th year of marriage which are supposed to be auspicious. Except the traditional or regular marriages, no elaborate ceremonies are observed. Besides this form of marriage a Kol can acquire a wife by marrying a window or divorced woman, by kidnapping or by abducting a widow or a married or unmarried girl.

All the disputes regarding the Kols marriage, moral lapses and irregular alliances are settled by the Panchayat. If any woman is involved in amorous intrigues the Tribunal Chaudhari or Mukhia settles the matter by negotiations. If she sexually indulges with a non-tribal person then the matter is viewed differently. The tribal Panchayat takes action against that woman or imposes some fine or 'bhoj' on her parents, or outcaste her.

## Religion

Religion plays a dominant role in the life of Kols. Their life is full of beliefs, superstitions, magic, rituals and festivals. They believe that they live in the midst of spirits, ghosts, phantoms and invisible beings who shape their destiny and course of life in a mysterious way. They are still believer of an animistic cult. But their religious life is greatly influenced by the Hinduism. Besides their gods and goddesses, they also worship Krishna, Shiva, Parvati, Indra and Hanuman because they believe that Sevari whose descendants they are was a devotee of God Rama. But their devotion to their own gods and deities is deeper. They worship a number of local gods which vary from village to village and region to region.

The most popular gods are Bhairon, Durga, Bhavani, Baradeva, Bhuiyar, Dulha-dev, Bhagat baba, Garaiya, Birhababa, etc. They also pay regards to female deities such as Kali, Phulmati Devi, sharda Devi, Nikshi, Dakshini etc.

Each Kol village has an open air temple which is marked by a mud platform, a few stone images and a flag staff. On special occassions, coconuts, beatles, 'batasha', 'malida' and 'root' are offered to the deities. Liquor is also offered to the deity and the rest is served among themselves as 'prasad'. Some benevolent and malevolent deities are propitiated with sacrificial offerings of goats, pigs or cocks.

On the Ramnavami day, celebrated on the ninth day after 'Amavayas' in 'Chaitra' (April-May) all sects of Kol community celebrate a periodical festival with pomp and show. They worship their deities especially Dulhadev.

They have also faith in Hindu religious functions and mythology such as Satyanarayan Katha, Kirtan, Ramayan and Gita.

The Kols are staunch believers in the spirits, called 'bhut' 'pret'. Ojhas are summoned for treatment who drives away the spirits in an extra ordinary manner. Some of the old coins ill-reputed for practising witch-craft and evil eyes which often causes harm, illness and even death to persons.

There are several types of superstitions prevalent among the Kols which are real taboos. Some superstitions are as follows:

(1) On 13th day (Teras) of each fortnight, they do not work in stone quarry centres.

(2) On 'Pariwa' or first day of the new year, they do not touch wood.

(3) On 'Amawas' or the last day of the dark half of the month, Kols do not work in the jungles.

(4) On journey, if a jackal crosses the path, he places a stone on the way or throws a piece of stone and then starts his journey.

(5) The women folk do not work on cultivated land in the

month of Jeth (May-June).

(6) On the day of Dipawali women do not go to work.

## Festivals

The Kols life goes round the festivals and ceremonies. Really, the festivals are part and parcel of their religions which is associated with the recreations and worship of their deities. They celebrate all Hindu festivals viz., Dussehra, Diwali, Holi etc. with special modification according to their customs and traditions. Although the main Hindu festivals are celebrated with great rejoicing, dancing and singing, Nau Durga and Ramnavami are performed in unique manner accompanied by dancing and witchery plays.

On the ninth day of the second fortnight or Kunwar (Oct-Nov.) goddess Durga or Bhavani is worshipeed. On the first day of 'nav-ratri' barley seeds are sown in the earthen post (tiles) which grow sufficiently in nine days. These are called 'jawaras'. On the ninth day 'jawaras' are taken out in a procession in the evening to the abode of the Devi. In the procession some of them get their cheeks, arms, necks and lips piered by an iron rod called 'sang' which remain stuck inside the body till they reach the place of Devi. On this occasion the Kols consider that goddess will fulfil the desires of the devotees.

## Recreations

Although the tribal life is full of worries and miseries, in short spells, they forget all in the chorus of melodious songs and thrill of robust dances. Singing, dancing, playing instrumental music and gossiping are the popular pastime among the Kols. Kabaddi, gulli-danda and wrestling are very popular among the young men. During the festivals, marriages and Devi-Puja they sing and dance. When a woman dances, the men play on dhol, nagara, manjeera etc.

## Welfare Programme

The state governments have taken several necessary test works during the three successive Five Year Plans to uplift the backward and depressed Kols. But they fail to acquite their goal due to the apathetic attitude of the Kols and discontinuity of the welfare schemes. During the first and Second Twelve Five Year Plans Rs. 43,000 were utilized for the construction of 43 Kol houses and Rs. 23,650 were disbursed among 67 Kols for cottage industry purpose. In both the Plane the first attempt was made to improve their housing and economic condition.

But is the Third Five Year Plan, U.P. Government prepared special schemes for welfare of the Tribals according to the Scheme prepared by the Government of India. During the Twelve Five Year Plan the following programme was chalked out and expenditure incurred on these heads :

During this plan 12 Kol colonies were set up in Manikpur and Mau blocs under the rehabilitation schemes and 233 Kol families out of 3978 families were given facilities for lodging.

## Table - 18

## Kol Colonies under the Rehabilitation Scheme in Chitrakoot District (2020)

| Name of Block & Tahsil | Name of village where the colony is situated | No. of houses built | Land given to inmates in Hectares |
|---|---|---|---|
| Manikpur (Tahsil) | Murkata | 15 | 30 |
| | Khichri | 32 | 64 |
| | Chheria | 15 | 30 |
| | Dondamafi | 8 | 32 |
| | Unchadih | 20 | 40 |
| | Sarhat | 22 | 44 |
| | **TOTAL** | **112** | **240** |
| Mau (tahsil) | Manka | 10 | 20 |
| | Kalchhia I | 15 | 30 |
| | Kalchhia II | 18 | 36 |
| | Kalchhia III | 20 | 40 |
| | Kaniyar | -- | 40 |
| | **TOTAL** | **63** | **166** |

Under this scheme an assistance of Rs. 3000 is provided as a whole to a Kol family which spends on the following items :

| | |
|---|---|
| (1) The construction of hutment | Rs. 1500. |
| (2) Reclamation of land | Rs. 250. |
| (3) Construction of Bundhies | Rs. 500. |
| (4) Purchase of a pair of bullocks and agricultural implements. | Rs. 510. |
| (5) Maintenance Grant for 6 months. | Rs. 240. |
| | **Rs. 3000.** |

A scheme of adult literacy for both men and women was undertaken by the Village Level Workers and Gram

Sevikas in the colonies but has been discontinued. In some of the colonies poultry programmes were introduced but has not proved successful.

In view of all these facts it can be assumed that the rehabilitation programme has made some impact on the socio-economic life of the Kols. Those Kols families living in colonies have better status in the tribal society than the others. It however, remains a fact that largely because of dishonesty and malpractices they could not get the full advantage of the scheme.

## Christian Missions Welfare Work

In the tribal areas the Christian Missionaries are also playing a significant role to promote the cause of the depressed class of the society. These institutions have provided educational, medical services and food stuff in bad times.

In Patha area there are two missions functioning. The Roman Catholic Mission is situated at Pakdilpur (Ranipur) nearly 18 Kms. south of Manikpur in thick forest, where the Kols live in good number. The other St. Rita's Own Italian Mission is situated at Manikpur. Both the Missions run educational institutions and dispensaries for the poor. These Missionaries also provide shelter, food, clothing and other necessities to the poor, old and orphans.

During the natural calamities the catholic Relief Society and the Ram Krishan Mission also provide a temporary relief to the Kols by distributing clothes, food grains, medicine, bedding etc.

## Problems and Suggestions

Poverty is the root cause of their backwardness. So their problems are numerous. The main problems which they experience are :

(1) The Kols live in debt and die in debt. Indebtedness leads to forced labour.

(2) They get very low wages from the non-triblals.

(3) The appalling illiteracy prevails among the Kols,

(4) By the ever-increasing restrictions of Forest Policy they have lost their hunting grounds as well as the source of income.

(5) The lack of transport and communication lines is largely experienced in the tribal areas.

(6) The medical facilities are totally inadequate.

(7) The scarcity of drinking water is another problem of tribal areas in the peak of summer months.

(8) Social corruption is greatly experienced by the Kols, because on a large scale their women folk work in forests, farms and homes. Young Kol girls often succumb to trifling temptations by the unscrupulous persons.

These problems can be tackled by the adoption of the following measures :

(1) It is necessary to cancel their past debts and to regulate the future money lending schemes.

(2) To educate their children, 'Ashram type of schools should be opened in the tribal areas. By persuading them that their children should be kept in these institutions, away from their parents.

(3) In the forest and mining and quarring works a special preference should be given to the Tribals.

(4) Their wages must be fixed by the government.

(5) Drinking water schemes should be carried out in tribal areas.

(6) More medical and educational centres should be

planned for the tribals. A mobile dispensary would be more useful for their treatment. Their medical treatment shouldbe free of cost.

(7) The area is badly in need of the metalled roads and bridges.

(8) As the area is sufficiently riach in raw materials, forest based small industrial units should be set up by the government on cooperative lines. Co-operative farming and forest co-operative societies will be very useful for the tribals. In this way the profit will not go in the pockets of the contractors but will be distributed among the labourers.

(9) To balance their economy it is essential that they must be supported continuously at least during the next Five Year Plans with sufficient aid.

# 19

# Human Morphology

Bundelkhand was never brought under the sway of Muslim rule for a longer period, therefore, the present Muslim population is either migrated from the other parts of the country or are converted from the Hinduism. Perhaps owing to this fact a section of Muslim population is called 'Muslim Rajputs'. In earlier years of their conversion their customs, traditions and rituals were quite similar to that of the Hindus and their societies were confined to the region. But is course of time they became staunch followers of the Muslim faith and social norms. The percentage of the Muslim is sufficiently higher in U.P. Bundelkhand than in M.P. Bundelkhand. In M.P. Bundelkhand their population was increased to 40766.

The social structure of the regional society is the prototype of Northern India's. Traditionally that is firmly based on 'Chatur Varna' (Colours, but not races) of the Hindu Society. For a time the Hindu society was divided on functional basis which 'represented nationality, common residence, religious distinction, occupations and cultural status as stated Ghurye, G.S. But as the time passed by the feeling of ritual ranking took the shape 'jati' (caste system).

## The Upper Castes

This group includes the Brahmins; the Kshatriya, and the Vaishyas of the Hindu society. In order of social precedence the Brahmins are at the apex of the social pyramid. Originally they migrated from Kannauj and were divided into two main branches - Kanyakubja (Kannaujia) and Yajur Gotra or Jijhotia. In local tradition Jijhotia sect is derived from the name of Raja Jujhar Singh who had got settled in his territory.[4] Other Brahmin groups viz., Sanadhya, Gaur, Sarwaria, Karwaria, Marwar, Dixit, etc. emigrated from time to time from other neighbouring parts of the country.

The Vaishyas have been placed third in the first society. Actually they are traders and businessmen and money-lenders. Economically, they are well-to-do. Jains are the sub-section of the Vaish group who are numerous in Jhansi and Lalitpur districts. The historical monuments of Deogarh reveal their past glory. In local tradition Depot and Khopat were two Jain brothers who possessed the philosopher's stone. By the help of the stone of the stone they amassed great richer and erected the fort and the town at Deogarh (Lalitpur). They are still rich enough and are religious minded. They observe their own customs, traditions, festivals with the Hindus.

## The Clean Castes

Except the scheduled castes, all the remaining Hindu castes are included in the clean caste group. A tendency has been marked among the clean castes to improve their social and economic levels in the hierarchy. "Wealth the weight, political or otherwise work as mighty levellers of sub-castes".

The clean castes can be divided into two main group:

(1) Agrarian, (2) Artisan. The Kurmi, the Lodhi, the Ahir and the Kacchi, are the excellent cultivators of Bundelkhand. In Banda, Hamirpur, Jalaun and Jhansi districts majority of them gains prosperity of the above agrarian castes. The artisan group includes Nai (Barbar), Kumhar (Potter man), Lohar (Blacksmith), Teli (Oilman), Bari (Bellman), Kahar (waterman), Sonar (Goldsmith), Darzi (Tailor) and others. They are incumbent on the agrarian society. They help the peasants by all means and get their wages in kind. Though hereditary professions are being practised by them. 'Socially the caste system antagonises the principles of equality among man and sects definite limits to mutual co-operation'.

## The Unclean Castes

The people of theses castes are engaged in menial works and are considered 'polluted' or untouchables. The group includes Dome, Basor, Dhobi, Chamar, Kuril, Pasi, Kori. Beldar, Badia etc. They return one third of the total population of Bundelkhand. In social behaviour they are at the bottom of the picture. Their social position is full of hardships, restrictions and denials. Sitting on cot is prohibited before the other castes. Their brides cannot ride on 'Palki; (Palanquin). The untouchables especially Dome is prohibited to enter the temples or sacred places and the well platforms. They are employed in 'begar' (forced labour). They are hesitant to and afraid of wearing golden ornaments and fine clothes. The chamar is agriculture labour class among the unclean castes. People of other castes are the traditional workers. In modern era the unclean castes have amended their hereditary traditional works by education and social reforms.

In appearance they are small and medium in stature and dark in complexion. They live in debt and die in debt. Panchayat (Council) is a powerful tribunal which controls their social behaviour. In the light of education and march of time, they are gaining momentum in socio-economic development. In the public services like rails, buses, hospitals, schools, etc. they are leading towards social equality. However, everywhere in the society 'caste' is taken into account and returns had results especially for scheduled caste peoples. The wealth and power are incapable to change the caste system of the Hindu society. Ratzel (F), 1898 has pertinently remarked that "in India countryman is a determining element and the life of the people cannot be understood apart from the religion and the social organisation with which it is entwined, often enshrined, and in both caste, is assuredly the most potent force and most immovable law". Gradually the social ties in Bundelkhand are loosing day by day and the scheduled caste people are penetrating into other walks of life as against the traditional occupations. After the independence they avail all opportunity of reservation in government services therefore their social Status is lifting by & large.

## Chief Characteristics of the People

The people of Bundelkhand are people of 'self-respect'. The feelings of revenge and retaliation go on from generation to generation. By appearance they seem rude and rustic but are quite hospitable. They lack moral courage and perseverance and fall pray to unscrupulous opponents. The pole with spear or some such thing which they hold, apprised about the salient features of their personality. Physically they are healthy robust and good looking. They speak plain and rude form of pure and mixed 'Bundeli' dialects, which is strident to hear. Their physical structure, complexion, dress and behaviour change according to the social hierarchy and gradation of socio-economic status. Higher castes are more refined than lower castes. They are inclined towards religious activities such as pilgrimage, study of holy books and solemnity. Natural catastrophes have made them orthodox, superstitious and fatalistic. 'Indolence, so patent from the difficulty of obtaining labour at any time, apathy so manifest in the face of calamity and helplessness so much in evidence in times of stress are undeniable characteristics of the people'.

They are habitual of mutual bickerings and litigations among them. A lot of money is spent of litigation. Theft, decoity, murder cases are very common. Illiteracy is the root cause of all evils which is a great obstacle in the regional planning and development. Both the rich and the poor are 'addicted to display on some occasion as marriages often indulge in much improvident extravagance'. They are very fond of wrestling and health-making. In every local fair wrestling matches are arranged. The historical and natural circumstances are more responsible for their mental make-up, habits of life which make them hostile to steady and persistent effort. However, the people of Bundelkhand are industrious, courageous and tolerant, but not ambitious.

Bundeli of western Hindi is chiefly spoken in the region and the neighbourhood. It is spoken by the uneducated and semi-educated people both of rural and urban areas. In the east of Banda district a mixed form of Bundeli and Bagheli dialect is spoken by the inhabitants. In the north of the Yamuna is the dividing line of Awadhi and Bagheli between Fatehpur and Banda districts. In the west of the region Bundeli is much influenced by the Gwaliori dialect, which is spoken in the west of Jhansi, Datia and Bhind districts. But in the south its extremity is broadened beyond the Sagar and Damoh districts. The total Bundel speaking population in India is 68.69 lakhs.

Bundeli is full of heroic tastes. The pronunciations are violent and very strident. It frequently puzzles the residents of the Doab (Ganga-Yamuna) not only from the variation introduced into the termination of nouns and verbs and the regular use of diminutives, but from the common use of words which are probably of the Gond or the other non-

Aryan Origin. Phonologically the words in Bundeli are the lengthening of the final syllable of many ordinary Hindi words e.g., 'Chakki' to 'Chakiya', 'Khat' to 'Khatiya'. Nasalised sounds are prominent, the 'jaise' of Hindi becomes the 'jaisen' of Bundeli.

Pure Bundeli is spoken in the region between the Dhasan and the Betwa river. It has a literature dating from the time of Chhatra Shal of Panna and his immediate predecessors of the early part of the eighteenth century. The most popular folk-epic off northern India the 'Alha-Khand' of Jaganik is written in the Bundeli language in Devanagari scripts. The epic commemorates the heroic deeds of Alha and Udal, the fortunes of Mahoba and its (Mahoba) capture by Prithvi Raj of Delhi. 'Banafar' is spoken in the south-east part of Bundelkhand including Mahoba, Charkhari, Laundi, Ajaigarh and Chhatarpur tehsils where Banafar Rajputs (Alha-Udal - Malkhan etc.) resided. It resembles the eastern Hindi but with an emphasis on Bundeli. 'Lodhati' is a pecular local dialect of Lodhis. It is very rude and rough 'boli' of Bundeli which is spoken mainly in Orai, Rath and Garautha tahsils where majority of Lodhi population resides. Tirahari (the boundary dialect) is spoken along the banks of the Yamuna including northern parts of Bhind, Jalaun, Hamirpur and Banda districts. It differs a little from pure Bundeli due to the influence of Awadhi dialect. And Bhadauria is chiefly spoken in Bhind and Jalaun districts.

### Dress and Ornaments

The dress and the ornaments are the index of the social economic life of the people, climatic requirements and traditional pattern of the region.

The hot climatic conditions of the region do not change much the dresses of the people. They wear the cotton fabrics throughout the year. In the winter months the well-to-do section of the society wears the wollen fabrics. However, the poor use the same clothes of coarse and cheap varieties of power loom fabrics only in exceptional cases they use the woolen sweaters, coats. 'Safi' (a little turban) is wrapped on the head for the protection against shivering cold at night.

Nothing is distinctive about the dress of the regional people as prevalent in northern India. But the style and mode of wearing is significant to note from one part to another. Generally the dress of the male consists of 'dhoti', 'kurta' or shirt, 'Panhi' (shoes) and 'Safi' (small turban) and female dress- 'dhoti' or 'saree' and 'Jhoola' or blouse. The quality of the clothes differ according to the standard of living. The rich men mostly wear the fine fabrics.

In M.P. Bundelkhand women folk wear their 'saree' or 'dhoti' - somewhat a man's 'dhoti'. The lower portion of the 'saree' is taken between the legs and tucked into the waist band at the back. In the rural areas the 'dhoti' are worn by women in various dark shades of red and catechu colours. They use the countrymade blouse without bodice. Such style of wearing the garments is very common among the low caste women folk who are engaged in field works or out door labour.

Necklaces, earrings and anklets of different shape and size made of silver and gilt are worn by women. Married women wear several ornaments of different variety.

In the west of Datia, Jhansi and Bhind districts women put on a 'lehnga' or 'ghagra' (long loose skirt) with a 'choli' (Tied blouse) and a loose flowing garment called 'loongda' or 'Orhani' or 'faria' (long scraf) which is tied over the 'ghagra' in front and taken over the breasts via hips which are covered. A little portion of 'loongda' covers the head and face. It is made of cotton fabrics in dark favourite mahroon, green and yellow colours. 'Lahnga' is narrow at the top and has a bigger circumference at the bottom. It is tied at the navel by means of a strong string. It is prepared with the thick cotton cloth of gaudy colours. No under-wear and bodice are used with this garment. It is the ancient costume as the Khajuraho sculpture shows. Belgar an eminent historian describes the dress and ornament of the ancient women that 'a petticoat from the waist down wards closing in front with a bunch or ornamental knob hanging down from the back a short way and ornamental bedwork. A long piece of cloth, used as a wrapped or saree with the end looped up. Such dress is still largely used by the backward castes but some of them seem to have overcome from the traditional garment replacing with saree, blouse and petti-coat. Women wear very heavy silver ornaments, on different parts of the body. The following silver ornaments e.g., 'Khangoria', 'bara' and 'Paizana', are very popular among the women folk who wear on neck, arms and anklets respectively.

## Tattooing

Women are very fond of decorating their body with ornaments, paints and tattooing. Tattooing is very popular mode of decoration among the women folk. All females, rich and poor in both rural and urban areas get tattooed. It is usually carried out before the marriage, between the age of 8 and 12 years. Apart from the decorative importance an old woman states the following justification for tattooing :

## Food and Drink

'Bejhar' (mixed form of barley gram and wheat gram) and Jowar-Bajra are the staple food grains of the people. Rice is eaten mainly in rice producing areas. In the southern upland which is less fertile coarse grains like rally Fikar, kakun, kodo etc are chiefly eaten by the poors. In the plains mixed form of grains are consumed by the majority.

The diet of the villagers is ill-balanced due to the preponderance of cereals. The percentage of protein is inadequate in the poor man's diet. Therefore, malnutrition, which affects the health. Clean castes are generally vegetarian while the uncleaned castes are treated as non-vegetarian. Interdining is practised according to the rules. Roughly, those castes dining together are treated as of equal status. Brahmins accept water and pucca food (cooked by oil and ghee) from a few castes. It is a fact that there is a wide difference in ritual ranking. A very few member of different castes at together due to caste bindings.

On the festive occasions like marriages and other festivals the feasts are largely elaborated. Speciality and peculiarity of food depends on the socio-economic status of the people. The food served by the Brahmins, the Kshatriyas and the Vaisyas in marriage differs from that of the Ladies, the Kurmis and the lower castes. The clean castes take the 'Kachcha' food in the kitchen after the bath but uncleaned castes are not regular in daily practices. As a rule male eats first and the women follow.

## Social Customs

A number of ceremonies are observed at the birth of male child in every caste. During the eclipse the expectant mother is not permitted to see the sun or the moon. On the birth a child the famiy members are considered ritually impure. No offering or 'puja' (sacrifice) is performed in the 'Chhatti' ceremony is observed in consultation with the priest. After twelve days of birth 'namkaran sankar' (Christening) is performed. On this occasion house is cleaned and a dinner is given to the relatives and friends. But in the case of the baby being a girl, these ceremonies are not performed on an elaborate scale.

'Upnayan Sanskar' is only observed among the 'dwij' (twice born) castes of the Hindu society. Other clean castes have also started wearing the sacred thread. Marriage is a sacrament and a common feature among the Hindus. Its rites differ from caste to caste and from region to region, which are sanctioned by customs and tradition. Among the backward castes child marriage is customary but in clean castes adult marriages are prevalent. Negotiated marriages are common. 'Sapinda' marriage are prohibited both by law and customs. Dowry system is very common among the high castes, as well as the low castes. 'Barat' (marriage party) generally goes by bullock carts and tractors in rural areas. The number of the members and bullock carts depend on the socio-economic status of the master. They beautiful their bullocks and carts with colours and coloured cloth. Then the 'Barat' marches with pump and show. The clean castes use 'Palki' or 'Doli' for the bride and bridegroom but unclean castes do not. Marriages are performed according to their culture and religion. In march of time all the marriage systems are getting change generation to generation.

The post marriages are also very common but widow marriages and 'gharbaitha' marriages are practiced only among the backward communities. It is significant to note that in a caste or a sub-caste, group of families marry only among themselves. This principle of endogamy is the only sure criteria of a particular caste or sub-caste. In a limited circle they extend their affinity with each other. If they take bride from a group they will not marry their sisters or girls in that group. In this way they maintain the 'Sapinda' marriage system.

**Fairs and Festivals**

They play an important socio-cultural role in the Hindu society. Festivity is also essential to entertain the human beings. Without them all the activities would become monotonous. Fairs and festivals draw together the people of neighbourhood and community ties are strengthened by common participation. They also offer opportunities for buying and selling the commodities because they attract the merchants, artisans and group of businessmen at a particular time and place.

Festivals are of many kinds- some of them are connected with eclipse, gods and local festivals which are observed by the people during the annual calendar.

'Raksha Bandhan' is one of the important festivals of Bundelkhand which is celebrated on the full moon day in the month of 'Shravana' (August) with great rejoicing. Wrestling bouts are arranged in every village. Women sing 'Kajari' folk songs. Swinging is a customary part of the festival. A special 'Kajari Mela' is held at Mahoba at the banks of Kirat Sagar every year at this time. The sisters tie 'rakhis' on the writs of their brothers reminding their duties to help their sisters in times of difficulty.

'Nav-ratra' is colourful festival of Bundelkhand which is celebrated twice in a year - Ist to 9th day of the bright half of 'Chaitra' (April) and 'Asvina' (September). On this occasion especially the middle and low classes participate and worship the goddesses Durga, Kali, Bhawani, Bhairav for nine days in a particular place. In the last day a procession in taken out, which is called 'Jawara' in both the rural and urban areas. They arrange some witchcraft and dances in this colourful procession.

In the land of Chandelas and Bundela's 'Dussehra' is observed in the month of Kartik (October) with great pump and enthusiasm. In this auspicious occasion the regional people not only commemorate the good deeds of Sri Ram but also they keep in memory the heroic works of the Chandela and the Bundela Rajputs who sacrificed themselves for the cause of the native land against the invaders.

Sri Ram had passed a few years of his exile at Chitrakoot hence he was well acquainted with the society of Bundelkhand. Ram Lila is performed at different places in the memory of Ram and on the last day Ravan of Lanka is beheaded. In the evening after taking delicious food they embrace each other forgetting all the internal ill-wills. As gift they give the 'Pan (betel) as a sign of amity.

Diwali (festival of light) is also celebrated in a unique manner in the region which falls on the Kartika Amavasya. In commemorates Rama's victorious return to his capital from exile of 14 years. Every one appears in jubilant mood on this occasion. The houses are white washed and cleaned and illuminated with the small earthen lamps. In the evening the farmers, businessmen and other workers worships their implements and working tools. Popularly Lakshmi (Goddess of wealth) and Ganesh (god of wisdom) are worshipped in every house. In the same night some people indulge in gambling. In the next day of Diwali, 'Govardhan Puja' is performed by the women folk and complete holiday is observed by the people.

A procession of 'Manisha' (dumb people) is carried in this day. They worship the village deities especially the cow. They observe fast the whole day and drink water just like cow. Without shoes and taking a bunch of 'More Pankh' (Peacock feather) in hands, they drive away the cows form place to place for free grazing. Such processions are carried out in every village of the region. In the evening they break their fast. The animals are also made to take a dip and their bodies are coloured and they are well fed on this occasion. This day has a special significance for the Jains because their twenty-fourth 'Tirthan Kara-Mahavira', attained nirvana on this day.

Holi is a popular festival of the Hindus. It is observed on the full moon day of 'Phalguna' (March). It is known as the festival of colours. It provides a lot of fun and revelry and has a strong appeal for the younger folks. Every one appears in jubilant mood. The ladies are also equally enthusiastic in celebrating the Holi festival among equally enthusiastic in celebrating the Holi festival among themselves. 'Phag' (festival song) party visits door to door in the villages. Every section of the society freely participates in the procession. They embrace each other forgetting mutual bickering. Liquor (country made wine) and 'bhang' (cannabis sativa) and freely distributed and used in this festival.

Other important Hindu festivals Ram-Naumi, Nag Panchami, Janamashtami, Makar-Sankranti, Shivratri, Basant Panchami, etc. are celebrated by the people. The Muslims celebrate their own festivals e.g., Moharram, Ramzan, Idul-fitr, Id Uz-zuha, Barawafat, Shabe-barat, Milad Shareef etc. In the rural areas they do not appear so rigid about their socio-religious practices. Mostly they lead simple life as the Hindus because their numbers is small and they are the sons of the same soil.

The peasants observe special ceremonies regarding agriculture, 'Asadi Parewa' (First day of the Hindu month) is considered the first working day of the agriculture calender. So they observe complete holiday on this days. To see fish on this day is considered a good omen for the peasants. Before sowing and harvesting several ceremonies are observed by them. After consulting the 'purohit' (priest) they start the agricultural works.

# 20

# General Background

Bundelkhand soils vary from rich black cotton soil to immature stoney soils. But satisfactory responses are only possible through the proper soil management and irrigational facilities. Soil erosion is a serious problem of Bundelkhand which has adversely affected agricultural economy. It necessitates immediate suitable soil conservation practices.

The region is rich in mineral deposits except the Panna diamonds, others have local importance due to low production and lack of industrialisation and transportation. An intensive geological survey is needed because Bundelkhand lies in central geological belt of India which has ample mineral wealth.

Bundelkhand preserves valuable species of flora and fauna. The former varies from deciduous forests to thorny forests. The ravine belt is mainly covered with stunted shrubs and thorny bushes, while the Vindhyan ranges possess luxuriant monsoon deciduous forests. The riverine areas are uses for the stock raising and the Vindhyan forests provide valuable timbers of teak and other miscellaneous species like Tendu, Khair, Achar, Mahuwa etc. The local hills and hillocks are eroded-land, chiefly covered with vegetal bushes. The people have largely exploited the forests because these are the main source of raw materials for the forest based industries. Similarly they have also destroyed most of the rich faunal species by the brutal cutting of jungles and indiscriminate shooting. The conservation of 'green gold' and the wild life is urgently needed, so that the natural balance can be maintained.

In early period Bundelkhand was sparsely populated by the primitive tribes. But under the Chandela Rajputs the region enjoyed peace and prosperity and population increased far and wide. In the medieval period population fluctuated due to the war and fear of war and the rise of feudalism. During the British rule population expanded by and large due to the freedom from depredation and facilities of irrigation and communication.

The population remarkably decreased. the trend is upward which has resulted in a steep rise during. There is no problem of 'over population' in Bundelkhand. So far as its regional distribution and density (121 persons per Km.$^2$) is concerned, the agricultural density is low (187 persons per Km.$^2$) than the carrying capacity (651 persons per Km$^2$.). The region has still extensive areas which are sparsely populated and have further possibilities for the growth of population as well as production.

During the last two decades the increase of population and the family divisions have accentuated the requirements of the more houses in the rural areas and movement of population has created housing problems in urban areas. The rural as well as urban housing schemes are urgently needed in the Bundelkhand region, so that residential conditions may be improved

**Table – 19**

**Workers (2020)**

| S. No. | Dist. | Agriculture | House hold industry | Worker |
|---|---|---|---|---|
| 1 | Lalitpur | 18.5 | 5.5 | 39.3 |
| 2 | Jhansi | 44.6 | 2.8 | 20.7 |
| 3 | Jalaun | 50.6 | 3.4 | 26.4 |
| 4 | Hamirpur | 50 | 3 | 24.5 |
| 5 | Mahoba | 54.4 | 3 | 23.5 |
| 6 | Banda | 54.6 | 3 | 21.4 |
| 7 | Chitrakoot | 66.2 | 2.4 | 12 |

In the ancient period the primitive people did not make the permanent human settlements in this part of the country due to unstable life. However, the systematic colonisation began from the Chandela period. During the Medieval period the rural republics met with decay and disaster due to the political upheavals. Under the British rule 'Centrifugal took the place of centripetal' people began to move out of their village remparts in search of agricultural land and better living prospects. Bundelkhand is par excellence a land of villages which vary in size. Both the physical and culture factors have greatly contributed to the evolution and distribution of the rural settlements. A Typical studies of the villages as Prithvipur, Palra, Uncha and Ranipur have been taken into account to present a clear picture of settlement pattern land use pattern and social pattern in plateau and plain areas.

## Table – 20

## Niwari District (2020)

| Block | Km$^2$ | Density | Male | Female | Total | Urban pop. | Rural Pop. | Family Planning |
|---|---|---|---|---|---|---|---|---|
| Niwari | 447 | 305 | 98,079 | 86,603 | 1,84,682 | 7% | 93% | 876 |
| Prathvipur | 723 | 287 | 1,11,406 | 1,08,719 | 2,20,125 | 18.7% | 81.3 % | 1160 |

The Chandela period gave birth to the city culture in the Bundelkhand region. But in Medieval times the strategic location sites were the main attractive points of urbanism. The majority of modern Bundelkhand towns are over-grown villages. The growth trend is largely influenced by the topography, climate and economy. The total increase of urban population during the last seventy years is 107.3 percent recording nearly 13.43 percent of its total population is urban. The size of town varies from Class I to Class VI. Most of the towns are small to medium in size because of undeveloped of transportation, industrialisation and trade. According to functional classification there are 6 agriculture centres, 2 mining centres, 7 household industrial and manufacture centres, 3 trading centres, 2 transport centres, 7 service centres and 6 diversified centres. The potentiality of urban centres has been worked out : it varies on the basis of socio-economic indices from each class. Jhansi, Banda, Chhatarpur & Hamirpur urban centres have been selected for morphological study. Lastly, the umlands, of urban centres have been delimited.

Bundelkhand is basically an agricultural region. A large section of population depends on agriculture. However, it is backward to all intents and purpose. The cereals (92.3 percent) dominate the cropped area while non-food crops are insignificant. Dry farming is being practiced in about 84 percent of cultivated area. Mixed cropping pattern and traditional farming are the main features of the regional agriculture. According to land use pattern 8.40 percent under forest, 17.67 percent culturable waste land, 16.14 percent fellow land and 60.86 percent available for cultivation. Before the introduction of the canal systems tank irrigation was initiated by the Chandelas and Bundelas. In the Southern part tanks and wells are the main source of irrigation and the north-west and north-east areas are irrigated by canals. The total irrigated area (2020) is 60.86 percent of the cropped land out of which irrigation by wels and tubewells is 38.58 percent, by tanks and lakes 3.64 percent and the rest by canals. Bundelkhand is rich in livestock wealth, having about 10783977 heads. The animals supply not only milk, mutton, ghee and beaf but also raw material for the cottage industries. The region is a large exporter of 'ghee' The agricultural and cattle farms are rendering important sevices in the progress of scientific agriculture and cattle rearing.

Although Bundelkhand is rich in raw materials, yet it is industrially backward due to the lack of means of transport and communication, enterprise, technical assistance and skilled labour. Except a few large and medium scale units e.g., the Baidyanath Ayurvedic industry, Indian Hume Pipe Company and Spirit making industry, others are small scale industries, based on the local resources. These are catergorised into broad groups as food industry, textile industry, leather industry, metal works forest industry, stone works etc. The region has better prospects for flour (maida) mills, dal and oil mills, livestock industries, cardboard and straw board industries, rice brown oil mills, paper and pulp industry, timber sawing, wood working, lac industry and coal, katha and biri making industries. Besides, paints and varnish, glass works, insecticides and pesticides have also good scope for development.

## Table – 21

## Satna District Block vise Detail -(2020)

| Block | Km² | Population | Forest Area | Net Sown Area Hect. |
|---|---|---|---|---|
| Amarpatan | 652 | 1,88,005 | 12,704 | 38,320 |
| Ram Nagar | 601 | 1,33,393 | 9,393 | 24,373 |
| Rampur Baghelan | 874 | 1,62,618 | 7,389 | 58,250 |
| Maihar | 1125 | 2,94,539 | 30,649 | 52,738 |
| Unchehra | 897 | 1,60,016 | 40,264 | 32,945 |
| Nagodh | 916 | 2,00,254 | 19,375 | 52,783 |
| Satna (Sohwal) | 772 | 1,35,774 | 4,755 | 50,230 |
| Majhgawan | 1584 | 1,69,950 | 79,130 | 47,887 |

The backwardness and stagnation of the region is largely due to the inadequate means of tranportation and communication. Luckily the national highway Sagar-Jhansi-Kanpur passes through the region. The length of metalled and unmetalled roads is 12556 Kms respcetively. The roads on the plateau area are zig-zag and run up and down. The lack of road bridges causes serious interruptions. The rail length amounts to 4815 Kms.; all being broad gauge. For a long time Bundelkhand remained inccesible because of its physical built. But the introduction of railways and roads has enhanced its accessibility. The southern plateau area is suited for road transport. However, the northern plateau area needs more extension and construction of surfaced and unsurfaced roads.

The trade of the region is primarily based on the products of agriculture, livestock, forest and mineral wealth. With the increasing transportation and communication facilities growth of population and socio-economic development, the dimensions of trade have expanded. Exports are dominated by the produce of the fields and forests. The main export articles are cereals, pulses, oil-seeds, pan, ghee, hides and skins, bones, timber, kattha, tendu leaves and minor forest produces. In manufactured goods Ayurvedic medicines, paper, cardboard and handloom clothes dominate exports. Among emports the counsumer goods were predominant.

**Table – 22**

**Gwalior Distt. Detail Block Wise (2020)**

| Sr.No. | Blocks | Village |
|---|---|---|
| 1 | Dabra | 135 |
| 2 | Bhitarwar | 86 |
| 3 | Ghatigaon | 113 |
| 4 | Morar (Rural) | 118 |
| 5 | Morar (Urban) | 68 |

**Table – 23**

**Tribes of Bundelkhand (2020)**

| District Name | Tribes Name |
|---|---|
| Tikamgarh | Biar, Biya, Saur |
| Niwari | Sontua, Biar, Biya, Saur, Sawar |
| Chhatarpur | Saur, Sawar, Bedia, Sonta, |
| Satna | Danuk, Bhaini, Manjhasi |
| Panna | Bedia, Kol, Manjhasi, Mawasi, Agaria |
| Datiya | Danuk, Saharia |
| Gwalior | Bhil |
| Jhansi | Bhil |
| Chitrakoot | Kol |

During the thirteen Five Year Plan (2017 to Now) the U.P. Government chaked out an economic development plan and housing scheme to imporve their socio-economic conditions. Actually they are facing a number of problems in day to day life such as indebtedness, low-wages, illiteracy and lack of transportation, medical facility and scarcity of drinking water. These problems can be tackled by adopting the following measures :

1) Their previous debts should be cancelled and new money lending schemes be introduced.
2) To educate their children, 'Ashram' Type schools will be useful in the tribal areas.
3) Priority should be given to the tribals in forests and quarring centres.
4) Their wages should be fixed by the government.
5) Drinking water schemes, medical and educational centres should be planned in the tribal areas.
6) In these areas small industrial units based on forest resources also should e set up by the government on cooperative lines.
7) Forest co-operative societies and co-operative farming will be very useful for them.

# Bibliography


1. Agrawal, R.P. 'Bundeli Ka Bhasha Shastria Adhyan, Lucknow, 1963.
2. Agrawal, R.R. & Mehrotra, C.L., 'Soil Survey and Soil Work in U.P., Allahabad, 1952.
3. Ahmad, E. Rural settlement types in U.P. Annals, XLII, 1952
4. Ali , W.A. The Fauna of India, Asia, Rev. vol 25, 1930.
5. Alam, S.M., 'Hyderabad-Secunderabad (Twin Cities) : A Study in Urban Geography, Hyderabad, 1965.
6. Altekar, A.S., 'Prachin Bharat Shasan Paddhati', Bharti Bhandar, Prayag, Sv. 2004.
7. Atkinson, E.T., 'Statistical Descriptive and Historical Accounts of North-West Provinces (Bundelkhand), Vol. I, Allahabad, 1874.
8. Agricultural Systems of Distribution of Population, W. Europe, 1926-52.
9. Bhartendu Prakash (ed) "Problem and Potentials of Bundelkhand, with special reference to water base center for Rural Development," Delhi, 1998.
10. Broke, J.O.M. and Bebb, J.W., 'A Geography of Mankind', Mc-Graw Hill, New York, 1968.
11. Bharat Dogra (2009) climate change and massive distrese in Bundelkhand main stream vol-47 No. 6 24 Jan 2009.

12. Chaurasia, RA. Environment Geography, Kitab Mahal, Allahabad 1998.
13. Chandana, R.E 'A geography of population, Kalyan Publisher, New Delhi, 2010.
14. Champion, H.G., 'Indian Forest Records', Vol. I, Nol, Dehradun, 1961, pp.90.91.
15. Chaturvedi, S.R. Kalidas Gram thawali, IIed Kashi.
16. Crook, Sir W., 'The Tribes and Castes of N.W.P. and Oudh', Allahabad, 1891.
17. Cunningham, A., 'A Tour in Bundelkhand and Malwa in 1863-64 and of Malwa and Gwalior in 1884-85,', Arch. Report. Vol. XXI, Pt. I and II, Calcutta, 1885.
18. Cunnigham, A. 'Ancient Geography of India, London, 1963.
19. Demangeon, A. 'The Origins and Causes of Settlement Types', Readings in Cultural Geography, 1962. PP. 506-16
20. Dobby, E.H.G., 'Monsoon Asia', London, 1962.
21. Dubey, S.C., 'Indian Village', London, 1961.
22. Dwivedi, S.S. (ed) Vir singh Dev Charit, Allahabad, Sv. 2013.
23. Ford, C.D., 'Habitat, Economy and Society', London, 1949.
24. Garnier, J.B. 'Geography of Population, London, 1966.
25. Ghosh, N.N., 'Early History of India', Allahabad, 1951.
26. Ghurye, G.S., 'Caste and Class in India', Bombay, 1957.
27. Gurjar, Ramkumar & Jat, B.C., 'Water Resource Geography' Rawat Pub., New Delhi, 2007
28. Grierson, G.A., 'Linguistic Survey of India', New Delhi, 1967.
29. Gupta, B.D., 'Maharaja Chhatrasal Bundela', Agra, 1958.
30. Gupta, A.P. (1995) Bundelkhand ka Lok Jeewan Survey Report cultural Department/ Govt. of U.P. India.
31. Gupta, A.P. (1999) Sanskratic Bundelkhand Naman Prakashan – Orai.

32. Gupt, Narmada Prasad – 1995-Bundelkhand ki Lok Sankrit ka itihas, Radha Krishna Publication Delhi.

33. Gupt, N.P. (Sammat 2024 – Bundelkhand ka Simankan, Mamalia, Bundelkhand Sahitya Akadmi Chhatarpur, San.

34. Hasan, A., 'Kols of Patha', Allahabad, 1972.

35. Houston, J.M., 'A Social Geography of Europe', London, 1953.

36. Kanitkar and others, 'Dry Farming in India', ICAR, New Delhi, 1960.

37. Kanjilal, P.C., 'A Forest Flora for Pilibhit, Oudh, Gorakhpur andBundelkhand', Allahabad, 1933.

38. Kendrew, W.G. 'The climats of the continents, oxford, 1953.

39. Kayastha, S.L., 'The Himalayan Beas Basin : A Study in Habitat, Economy and Society', B.H.U., Varanasi, 1964.

40. Krishnan, M.S. Geology of India and Burma, Madras, 1960

41. Kumar, Pramila "Madhya Pradesh Eak Bhougolik Adhyan" hindi Granth Akadmi, Bhopal, 1994

42. Kumar, Pawan, "Water Resource Management and Agricultural Development Planning in Patha Tract of Manikpur, Chitrakoot District A.P.S. University, Rewa (M.P.), 2010

43. Kumar, Pawan, 'Dimension of Agriculture Development and environment Effects in Chitrakoot District, Ph.D Thesis A.P.S. University, Rewa (M.P.) 1915.

44. Lal, B. 'Mineral Wealth of Bundelkhand,' Allahabad University Marg 1970.

45. Law, B.C. (Ed.), 'Mountains and Rivers of India', NCG, Calcutta, 1968.

----------'The Rivers of India', N.C.G. Calcutta, 1968.

46. Majumdar, D.N., 'Races and Culture of India', Bombay, 1958.

----------"The Fortuner of Primitive Tribes, Lucknow, 1944.

47. Majumdar, R.C., 'The Vedic Age', London, 1951.

--------- " (Ed) 'The Age of Imperial Unity', Bhartiya Vidya

Bhavan, Bombay, 1953.

48. Memoria, C.B., 'Agricultural Problems of India', Allahabad, 1960.
49. Misra, K.C., 'Chandela Aur Unka Rajatvakal', Kashi, Sav. 2011.
50. Mishra, K.K. "Settlement Geography", Kusum Prakashan, Atarra (Banda) 1994.
51. Mukerjee, R.K. 'Man and this Habitation, London, 1940.
52. Neale, W.C., 'India : The Search for Unity, Demography and Progress', New York, 1965.
53. Newbigin, M.I., 'Plant and Animal Geography', London, 1957.
54. Nigam- M.L. (1983) Cultural History of Bundelkhand Laxmi Prakashan Jhansi.
55. O-Dell, A.C., 'Railways and Geography', London, 1956.
56. Oppert, G., 'Original Inhabitants of Bharatvarsa', Madras 1893.
57. Pandia, M.V. (Ed.), 'The Prathviraj Raso', Banaras, 1910.
58. Pandey, A.P., 'History of Bundelkhand (Under Chandelas), D.Phil. Thesis (Unpub.), Allahabad University, 1954.
59. Perpellou, A.V. 'Human Geography, London, 1966.
60. Patel, M.L. (Ed.), 'Agro-Economic Problems of Tribal India', Bhopal, 1972.
61. Powell, B.H.B. 'Indian Village Community, London, 1896.
62. Puri, G.S., 'Indian Forest Ecology', Vol. I, New Delhi, 1960.
63. Pandey, S.N. "Water Drought and Livelihood in Bundelkhand (2011)
64. Pandey, A.K. Bundelkhand ki Lok Paramparayan, 2008.
65. Polunin, N. 'Introduction of Plant Geography, London, 1960
66. Robertson, F.C.F, 'Our Forests', Allahabad, 1936.

67. Rao Rama, M.S.C., 'Soil Consevation in India', I.C.A.R., New Delhi, 1962.

68. Roychaudhari, S.P., and others, 'Soils of India', ICAR, New Delhi, 1963.

69. Ratzel, F. 'History of Mankind,' Vol. II, London, 1898.

70. Sankalia, H.D., 'Socio-Economic and Geographical Background of Khajuraho', Jou. Ind. His., vol, XLIX, Pt.I, 130, 1966.

71. Saxena, J.P., 'Geological Control on the Evolution of Bundelkhand Topography', Jou. of Geography, University of Jabalpur, Vol. II, No.2, 1960.

----------'Agriculture Geography of Bundelkhand', Ph.D. Thesis (Unpub.), Sagar University, 1967.

72. Shafi, M., 'Land Utilization In Eastern U.P.', Aligarh Muslim University, Aligarh, 1960.

73. Sharma, R.C. 'Settlement Geography of Indian Desert, New Delhi, 1972.

74. Sherring, M.A., 'Hindu Castes and Tribes', Calcutta, 1946.

75. Siddiqui, M.F.,'Physiographic Divisions of Bundelkhand', The Geographer, Vol. XIII, Aligarh, 1966.

76. Shafi, M. Agricultural Productivityand Regional Embalances A study of Uttar Pradesh, corcept Pub, New Delhi, 1983.

77. Smailes, A.E. 'Geographaphy of Towns, London, 1953.

78. Sen, Bandhudas, The Green Revolution in India, A Perspective New Delhi,1974.

79. Sankahia, H.D. "Socio-Economic and Geographycal Back ground of khajuraho, Jau. His. Bol.. XLIX Pt. /130, 1966.

80. Singh L.R. The Tarai Region of U.P. : A study in human Geography', Allahabad, 1965.

81. Singh, R.B., 'Transport Geography of Uttar Pradesh', N.G.S.I., Varanasi, 1966.

82. Singh, R.L., Banaras : A study in Urban Geography', Banaras, 1955.

83. Singh, R.L. (Ed.) 'India: A Regional Geography', N.G.J.I. Varanasi, 1971.

84. Singh, R.L. (Ed.) 'Rural Settlement in Monsoon Asia', N.G.S.I., Varanasi, 1972

85. Stamp, L.D. 'Our Developing World, London, 1960.

86. Smith V.A. 'Notes on the Bhars and other Early Inhabitants of Bundelkhand', Jon. Asi. Soc. Ben., Vol. 46, Pt. II, 1877.

87. Smith V.A. 'Contributions to the History of Bundelkhand', Jon. Asi. Soc. Beng., Part I, No.1, 1881.

88. Spate, O.H.K. and Learmonth, A.T.A., 'India and Pakistan', London, 1967.

89. Shriwastava Madu – (2006) Bundelkhand ki Lok Chitrakala.

90. Thornbury, W.D. 'Principles of Geomorphology, Newyork, 1954.

91. Tiwari, A.R., 'Geography of Uttar Pradesh', N.B.I., New Delhi, 1971.

92. Trewartha G.T. 'An Introduction to Climate', London, 1954.

93. Tripathi, B.P. "Bhartiya Krishi, Allahabad, 1992.

94. Tiwari, Rc & Singh, B.N. "Agriculture Geography Prayag Pistak Bhawan Allahabd, 2010.

95. Tiwari (G) (1990) Bundelkhand ka Sanchhipat Etihass P.45

96. Udo, R.K. 'Disintegration of Nucleated Settlements E Nigeria Geog. Rev. Vol. L.V., 1965.

97. Verma - B.L. Geography of Bundelkhand Raj Publication, New Delhi 2019.

98. Wagner, P.L. and Mikesell, M.W. (Ed.), 'Readings in Cultural Geography', The University of Chicago Press, 1962.

99. Weaver, John C., 'Crop-Combination Regions in the Middle West', Geog Rev., vol. XLIV, 2, April, 1954.

100. Wadia, D.N. 'Geology of India, London, 1961.

# Index